PRAISE FOR *EDUCATION ROADS LESS TRAVELED*

"Mitch Pearlstein is onto something very important: College education is not for everyone—but everyone should enter adulthood with a skill that can earn them a decent income, and help them support a family. If we are serious about making America into a country of prosperity for all, we need to give a serious listen to what Pearlstein has to say." —**Nicholas Eberstadt**, author, *Men Without Work: America's Invisible Crisis*

"Pearlstein has penned a timely and very useful book about why many people now find college to be more obstacle than opportunity. Notably, in an era when many are quick to demonize higher education or rush to its defense, he manages to do neither. Instead, he thoughtfully examines the landscape, suggests practical options, and sketches a promising path forward." —**Frederick Hess**, author, *Letters to a Young Education Reformer*

Education Roads Less Traveled

Education Roads Less Traveled

Solving America's Fixation on Four-Year Degrees

Mitch Pearlstein

ROWMAN & LITTLEFIELD
Lanham • Boulder • New York • London

Published by Rowman & Littlefield
An imprint of The Rowman & Littlefield Publishing Group, Inc.
4501 Forbes Boulevard, Suite 200, Lanham, Maryland 20706
www.rowman.com

6 Tinworth Street, London SE11 5AL, United Kingdom

British Library Cataloguing in Publication Information Available

Library of Congress Cataloging-in-Publication Data

Names: Pearlstein, Mitchell B., 1948- author.
Title: Education roads less traveled : solving America's fixation on four-year degrees / Mitch Pearlstein.
Description: Lanham, Maryland : Rowman & Littlefield, [2019] | Includes index.
Identifiers: LCCN 2018046347 (print) | LCCN 2018059076 (ebook) | ISBN 9781475847550 (electronic) | ISBN 9781475847536 (cloth : alk. paper) | ISBN 9781475852998 (paper : alk. paper)
Subjects: LCSH: Education, Higher—Aims and objectives—United States. | Education, Higher—Economic aspects—United States. | Educational change—United States. | Nontraditional college students.
Classification: LCC LA227.4 (ebook) | LCC LA227.4 .P43 2019 (print) | DDC 378.73—dc23
LC record available at https://lccn.loc.gov/2018046347

™ The paper used in this publication meets the minimum requirements of American National Standard for Information Sciences—Permanence of Paper for Printed Library Materials, ANSI/NISO Z39.48-1992.

With amazement and thanks for men and women who create, build, and fix things with their hands, especially since the only things I do with mine are type and eat.

Contents

Preface xi

Acknowledgments xiii

1 Lay of the Encouraging Land 1

2 The Four-Year-College Bias 21

3 Underemployed Paths to Great Jobs 35

4 The Growing Power of Debt 59

5 Potential Economic Detours 73

6 Potential Social Detours 85

7 The Art of Craft 99

8 Conclusion 111

Index 123

About the Author 127

Preface

Every year, large numbers of American young people who are not terribly interested in attending a four-year college reluctantly enroll anyway, effectively pressured by combinations of parents, peers, teachers, school counselors, and the normative air they breathe. More than occasionally, they wind up confirming that collegiate life is not for them and, sooner or later, drop out. From there, again more than occasionally, they find themselves unemployed or underemployed, in big-time student debt, and quite possibly feeling like a failure.

Cratered paths like these routinely stunt entries to middle-class jobs and careers. These are often needless delays and losses, because other education and career routes are primed to better serve millions of young men and women, especially those who enjoy working with their hands. Taking advantage of these routes also simultaneously enriches our economy.

Digging deeply into issues like these is the book's main aim. Helping teenagers think through what they want to do with their lives occupationally is its main educational mission. Recognizing the economic and other dangers posed by severe skill gaps, made worse by the retirement of millions of skilled baby boomers, adds urgency to the mix.

I've never dealt with an important issue in which consensus is so strong, and in which party affiliation and political ideology are seemingly so irrelevant, as is the case here.

Do Americans in the main believe that reducing vocational options in high schools was a mistake? Yes.

Do Americans in the main recognize that plumbers and electricians make good livings, and that job security for health care professionals such as paramedics and X-ray technicians likely won't weaken anytime soon? Yes.

Do Americans in the main believe that great numbers of young people would be happier and more successful if they pursued careers in the trades and other technical fields? Yes, albeit with the proviso that the young men and women in question are not their *own* kids, whom they see as mostly destined for four-year and perhaps graduate degrees.

And do Americans in the main recognize that an immense amount of work needs to be done on our nation's physical infrastructure, both adding to its stock and repairing what we have, and that people in construction and related fields are indispensable to these efforts and can get paid handsomely? Yes, once more.

None of this is to say disagreements and worries are absent in the pages that follow. Many Americans, for instance, perhaps older men and women of color particularly, are anything but nostalgic for the kinds of vocational education that used to limit rather than expand occupational and career choices for low-income students. They do not necessarily find talk of new and improved vocationally enriched education as reassuring as others might. The good news, though, is that older varieties of vocational education generally have been replaced by fairer approaches with more welcoming names such as "career and technical education," featuring more substantial and future-friendly curricula. We will examine issues like this in chapter 6, "Potential Social Detours."

In fact, rather than being an untextured paean to alternative education routes (or a sophomoric criticism of four-year institutions and degrees), the book doesn't shy away from other possible divots and boulders. This is most notably the case when it comes to whether women with B.A.s and J.D.s will be as romantically interested in men with A.A.s as they are in men with M.B.A.s. It's a tough question that warrants airing, particularly since it gets hardly any.

Caveats and qualifiers like these notwithstanding, *Education Roads Less Traveled: Solving America's Fixation on Four-Year Degrees* is an enthusiastic endorsement of the kinds of education routes, including apprenticeships and training in the military, that lead to the kinds of jobs that millions will find remunerative and satisfying and which our nation needs filled by highly skilled men and women. This last point is no small challenge.

Yet it's also no small opportunity, as the number of open jobs (as I write) is newly larger than the number of people seeking jobs. This is a new and stunning fact of economic life which, save for inevitable downturns, may last a long time. It surely would be a dreadful loss, in both personal and national terms, if too few people took advantage of it, both educationally and professionally. And not just men and women in their teens and twenties either.

Acknowledgments

Education Roads Less Traveled: Solving America's Fixation on Four-Year Degrees flows from Great Jobs Without a Four-Year Degree, a multiyear, ongoing project of Center of the American Experiment, the Minnesota think tank I founded with colleagues in 1990 and for which I served as president for almost all its first 25 years. My thanks to everyone associated with the Center, starting with teams of directors, staff members, and funders for more than a quarter-century of support and friendship, with an extra salute to those with whom I continue to work most closely on the Great Jobs initiative: John Hinderaker, Katherine Kersten, Catrin Thorman, Tom Steward, and Peter Zeller, among others. As for formatting the book, changing Roman numbers to Arabic ones in the endnotes, and other essential tasks that baffle me, my thanks to Pari Cariaga.

Even before its official start in 2017, Great Jobs Without a Four-Year Degree joined forces with other organizations and offices in a broader, private-public effort similarly aimed at ensuring that Minnesota has an adequate—make that superior—workforce going forward. Colleagues in this effort, in addition to Kathy and Catrin, include Scott Peterson, Mike McGee, Amy Walstien, and others. My thanks for their leadership.

Also animating the pages that follow were three events.

Being asked by D. J. (Doug) Tice of the (Minneapolis) *Star Tribune* to write an op-ed about whether we send too many people to college ("Yes," I answered with caveats). Sitting on a panel at the American Enterprise Institute with economist Robert Lerman, who spoke persuasively about the value of apprenticeships. And reading Matthew Crawford's fascinating *Shop Class as Soulcraft: An Inquiry into the Value of Work.* "Fascinating" because how can anyone not be fascinated by a writer who not only repairs exotic bikes but also hold a Ph.D. in political philosophy from the University of Chicago? My thanks to Messrs. Tice, Lerman, and Crawford.

I interviewed more than 80 people for the book, several of them several times. As is regularly the case whenever I interview dozens of men and women for a book or other project, I am most appreciative of interviewees' insights and candor, in what purposely resembled conversations more than formal interviews. More than 50 of the 80-plus sessions were recorded and then transcribed. I don't know how many different transcribers were involved in the lengthy exercise, but their turnaround times were exceptional. My thanks to everyone at Rev transcription services.

Early on I met with Kimberly Clarke, an excellent librarian at the University of Minnesota, as I sought to get a better sense of how our country's fixation on four-year degrees came to be. She was most hospitable and helpful, which didn't surprise me in the least, as I've always known librarians to be eager to help people track things down, perhaps the more elusive the better. Many more people, especially students, need to know this and take advantage of it.

Nevertheless, an admission. Given that spending time in the periodicals room at the University of Minnesota's Wilson Library was always something I looked forward to, other than my one or two visits with Kim, I never set foot into another brick-and-mortar library while writing this book, as Google and Bing seemed to handle all my bibliographic needs. My thanks to their people, too, I guess.

Keeping my computer and printer working so I could perpetually access Google and Bing were the mission-driven men and women at slash/Blue who remotely fixed what ailed my machines from wherever. Thanks for keeping me in business.

Tori Roloff, a student at the University of Virginia, was an intern of mine during the summer of 2017 who researched key issues and organized very useful roundtables. Suffice it to say she was impressive.

My gratitude likewise to economists Amanda Griffith at Wake Forest University and Nicole Brown at the Georgetown University Center on Education and the Workforce for their help with pivotal data. Gardner Gay, an old friend, wound up as co-champ with Tori in recruiting interesting interviewees (namely, a sizable portion of his own family). My large thanks to him, as well as to another old friend, Kent Kaiser, who did a first round of line editing and later constructed the book's index, two chores he has performed for me several times in the past.

The most immediate way *Education Roads Less Traveled* got going were two quick email exchanges on a Saturday early in 2017 with Rowman & Littlefield's Tom Koerner, an excellent editor with whom I had worked previously. I copied him that day on an email to someone else about something entirely different and he wrote back right away, saying it was good to hear from me and did I have another book in me? I responded right away saying, "Funny you should ask," as I was getting itchy to write a new one and I gave him a few paragraphs about how many young people would be better served if they considered education routes other than four-year degrees, especially if they like working with their hands. Tom got back just as fast and, save for the fact I had to write a real proposal and touch base with my American Experiment colleagues, we were on. This may be my proudest publishing story. My ongoing thanks to Tom, Carlie Wall, and others at R&L, especially since I may get itchy again in a year or two.

Finally, we've come to the Rev. Diane Darby McGowan, who has been at the center of my galaxy for decades but who, I fear, thinks I've been spacey and aloof again while completing a book. "Not true," I say. "No way." And on top of that, my beautiful wife, "I promise not to do it again."

Chapter 1

Lay of the Encouraging Land

Finally revved to begin this introduction, I did what I've been known to do when muses finally announce themselves: I turned on the TV instead. But as synchronized fortune would have it, the first show to pop up that Saturday afternoon was an *American Masters* portrait of the brilliant French American chef Jacques Pépin. Somehow, PBS had rewarded my procrastination, as the program's full title was "Jacques Pépin: The Art of Craft." Great perks evidently do come with being a sustaining member of Twin Cities Public Television.

What an intriguing term, worthy of quotation marks and capitalization: "The Art of Craft." Might it apply to what *Education Roads Less Traveled* is about? Yes, especially in the latter parts of the book. Also, acute in the pages that follow is recognition that millions of young Americans would be better off, financially and in other ways, if they seriously considered pursuing careers in fields where four-year degrees are not necessary. Prominent, too, is recognition that American prosperity relies much more on highly trained, technically talented men and women with two-year degrees and professional certificates than is routinely acknowledged.

For instance, in the specific matter of STEM fields (science, technology, engineering, and math) the Georgetown University Center on Education and the Workforce argues the "STEM supply problem" reaches beyond the need for men and women with bachelor's and advanced degrees.[1] "We also need more qualified technicians and skilled STEM workers in Advanced Manufacturing, Utilities and Transportation, Mining, and other technology-driven industries." Over and above this underutilization, the report argues that a "deeper problem" is a "scarcity of workers with basic STEM competencies across the entire economy," touching on virtually every industry. Think of this last point as a lack not of expertise but of basic STEM literacy.

I decided to write this book in February 2017, when its main themes already had achieved a fair amount of salience. As I currently update matters, it's May 2018 and I'm a few days away from writing the conclusion. In those 15 months, profiles for those themes and topics have grown significantly, as witness a near-flood of essays, columns, and news stories, all seeming to run within hours of each other, such as an article by Aaron M. Renn in *City Journal*, "Manufacturing a Comeback"[2]; an op-ed in the *Wall Street Journal*, "Not Everyone Should Go to College"[3]; and a feature in the (Minneapolis) *Star Tribune*, "Manufacturing Booms, but Labor Runs Dry."[4] This growing intensity, in fact, has reached a point where I'm anticipating bad dreams in which corrals of scholars and writers also are finishing books on the personal and societal costs of Americans' preoccupation with baccalaureates, and they're expecting to get their books out before mine.

Yet no matter how many other books are eventually released, required of this one is seriously dissecting assumptions and pursuing tough questions like these:

- Why is the notion that "everyone" should get a four-year degree so potent when I have met a grand total of one person in my life who really believed it, and that was in the 1960s when lots of ideas didn't make sense?
- What kinds of threats might automation pose for men and women who earn the very degrees and certificates the book commends?
- What does an accentuated interest in alternative education and career routes suggest about who might, or might not, eventually marry whom?
- What fears does a focus on what some mistakenly equate with dead-end "vocational education" provoke in groups and individuals who have been denied opportunity by it in the past?
- What do actual voices of dozens of students, parents, educators, business leaders, and public officials sound like and what do they say about this constellation of issues?

Dealing substantively with important issues was my aim in early 2017, and I would like to think I've made good on it.

None of what follows, I stress, are gratuitous slams at colleges and universities. While I certainly have problems with various aspects of their operations—tuition rates that are frequently more stratospheric than earthbound, for example, and their frequent lack of ideological variety and intellectual open-mindedness, most of all—I celebrate how American higher education frequently is the envy of the world. I also recognize and appreciate, though some might discount my view as rhetorical overkill, how institutions of higher learning have been pivotal to American civilization itself for a long time and how they remain so despite weakened tailwinds, frequently caused by their own poor navigating. I agree with economist Philip Trostel when he writes, "It is not overstatement to call the effect on earnings just the tip of the iceberg of the college-payoff iceberg. There are more benefits to college education beneath the surface than above it."[5]

More personally, when I think about how I've benefited from my collegiate life, I often think of a visit 30 years ago to the Museum of Modern Art in New York City. As I rounded a corner, I saw van Gogh's *Starry Night*. Within microseconds, I said to myself, "That's *Starry Night*. That's van Gogh. This is the Museum of Modern Art. That means this is the original. This is very exciting." And then I got doubly excited because I had gotten excited. "My liberal arts education," I concluded in my instantaneous conversation with myself, "had worked."

Personally again, I'm in the debt of Binghamton University, where I did most of my undergraduate work, and the University of Minnesota, where I did all my graduate work. As for the qualifier about spending "most," not all, of my undergraduate life at Binghamton, and once again in keeping with the non-four-year thrust of this book, I owe a great deal to a freshman-only program in Brooklyn with one of the least ivy-endowed names in American postsecondary education history: City University College Center at New York City Community College. I had spent my junior high school and senior high school years handing in assignments no better than irregularly but finally got my academic head in reasonable order at CUCC@NYCCC, making it a life-saver for me. I will always eagerly express my thanks to the City University of New York for rapidly organizing five such programs (I seem to recall) aimed at bailing out underperforming baby boomers like myself who had been squeezed out of more traditional institutions in the mid-1960s.

In regard to where this book fits in with the rest of my work, I have spent much of my career focusing on the debilitating prices paid by millions of people and society by our country's huge out-of-wedlock birth rates and high divorce rates.[6] A major reason for such high levels of family fragmentation, especially in regard to nonmarital births, is the immense number of "unmarriageable men," in sociologist William Julius Wilson's famously painful term—men who cannot hold jobs that can support a family in large part because of their lack of skills, both hard and soft.[7]

Yet that critical constituency, while attended to in coming pages, is largely different from the one emphasized. Most of the main players addressed here are, in fact, on schedule to graduate from high school, or they've already done so, and are likely at least considering a four-year degree. By contrast, the men coldly classified as "unmarriageable" often have not made it out of high school, with vexing questions about whether to pursue a B.A. not ranking high on their list of worries.

While high school grads generally possess actual or potential job skills, as slim as they may be, those who never graduate from high school or who are not on track to do so generally have weaker skills, starting with an inability to read, write, and compute adequately. Still, while this latter group is not the book's central concern, the kinds of educational, job, and career routes discussed here can be of service to them, too, as well as to their families. At some point, people in situations like these have to bring *something* to the table in terms of marketable skills in order to do the least bit well.

For that matter, issues examined here also can be helpful to older Americans, perhaps especially men and women considering major midcareer changes, be those possible moves voluntary or not.

Begged here are questions of mobility, and it's very good to know that significant numbers of alumni of community and technical schools are climbing more socioeconomic rungs, and doing so faster, than many alumni of four-year schools. This is to say they are making more money and will continue doing so. Similarly, large numbers of men and women with two-year degrees and others with two-year and one-year certificates will wind up on higher rungs than substantial portions of those who start but then drop out of four-year programs. We will return to essential matters of mobility and inequality.

A family story: Seven or eight years ago, I was asked by the commentary editor of the Minneapolis-based *Star Tribune* if I thought "we send too many people to college." I said yes, he said write it, and I did.[8] Shortly after the op-ed ran, I received an email from my brother Robert, a high-end hairstylist in Boulder, Colorado, which was one of the most satisfying responses I've ever received to a piece. He said how much he liked the column, which was nice to hear certainly, but more importantly he spoke of how he has always been very proud of his profession—a reasonably lucrative career for which he had attended a "beauty" school rather than a more esteemed institution of higher education. Without glibly mocking myself for effect, I often think of how my brother, without my mildly fancy degrees, has made many more people happy, women especially, than I ever have or ever will. His has not been an insignificant contribution in an already beautiful part of the world.

What kinds of jobs are we talking about? Economist Robert I. Lerman, perhaps the nation's most respected scholar when it comes to apprenticeships, writes about "middle-level occupations" and "jobs at intermediate levels of skill." His eclectic examples include the likes of respiratory therapists, carpenters, heavy vehicle maintenance specialists, and heating and air-conditioning professionals. Lerman has defined intermediate-level jobs as "positions between jobs that require very little training and jobs that require a university degree."[9] Or, as an interviewee put it, "Good jobs, even great jobs. Jobs with depth and potential. With decent wages, benefits, and long-term security."

The previously mentioned Georgetown University Center on Education and the Workplace, in 2017, defined a "good job" as one that pays a minimum of $35,000 (or $17 an hour) for full-time jobs for workers under age 45, and a minimum of $45,000 (or $22 an hour) for workers 45 and older.[10] Not particularly impressive, but note the qualifier "minimum" in both instances.

More specifically and better, the U.S. Department of Labor,[11] in 2016, estimated plumbers, pipefitters, or steamfitters to earn $26.94 per hour on average; electricians to earn $27.24 per hour on average; and boilermakers to earn $29.90 per hour on average.

Or in terms of "top-end hourly pay," plumbers, pipefitters, or steamfitters were over $45.53; electricians were over $43.47; and boilermakers were over $41.25.

In a book titled *Job U: How to Find Wealth and Success by Developing the Skills Companies Actually Need*, Nicholas Wyman lists a score of "well-paying, respectable" jobs not requiring four-year degrees—jobs such as electricians, master chefs, cardiovascular technologists, machinists, aircraft mechanics, auto technicians, dental hygienists, and welders.[12] The latter occupation, as you may recall, being the celebrated one Sen. Marco Rubio cited when he declared in a 2015 Republican presidential debate that students and the nation would be better off if we had more of them and fewer philosophers.

Kevin Fleming presumably is of similar mind. He's the creator of the creative animated video which contends that for every *one* job that requires a master's degree or higher, *two* jobs require a four-year degree, and *seven* jobs require a two-year degree or occupational certificate, with this near iron law, he says, destined to continue.[13]

For now, let me just tease Matthew Crawford's fascinating book, *Shop Class as Soulcraft: An Inquiry into the Value of Work*,[14] in which he convincingly writes that it regularly takes greater cognitive firepower to figure out what ails a motor or engine and then fix it than it does to perform many white-collar jobs for which a four-year degree (at minimum) is required. In scores of interviews and conversations I've yet to find anyone who disagrees with this. The fact that Crawford is the hands-on owner of a motorcycle repair shop as well as the holder of a doctorate in political philosophy from the University of Chicago affords him a certain standing on the question. We'll focus on working with one's hands in chapter 7.

What kinds of education routes make the kinds of jobs and careers just discussed possible? We just mentioned apprenticeships, which Professor Lerman has described in a fulsome but tightly written sentence.

> Skill development through apprenticeships is closely suited to the needs of employers and the job market, reinforces classroom learning with applications at the workplace, involves trainees in the production process, makes for a

> seamless transition from school to a career, provides trainees with a natural mentoring process, allows trainees to earn wages while gaining occupational mastery, applies to a wide range of occupations, requires less government spending than other education and training strategies, and generally raises the quality of workforces.[15]

Community and technical colleges are also central to the mix, both in terms of their awarding two-year associate's degrees in technical fields, including those in which licensing or certification is required, as well as one-year and two-year certificate programs in a wide variety of occupational areas in which licensing or certification is again often required. Examples might include cosmetologists, dental assistants, nursing aides, massage therapists, and certified inspectors for boilers, houses, and motor vehicles among other things.

Lerman's reference above to "the needs of employers and the job market" is a good place to note that for men and women who might have graduated during a recession, or lost a job during an economic downturn, the implication that employers are eager to hire rather than lay off can be disorienting. "You mean companies are actively *looking* for people, maybe even like me?" Yes, they are and will be, albeit with the proviso that men and women looking for interesting and good-paying jobs be adequately employable.

As surreal as it may sound to victims of the 2008 crash and other inhospitable periods, shortages of workers will pose bigger problems than surpluses of them, save for future recessions and threats of them. Frank Forsberg, a former United Way official who has focused on workforce development issues for a long time, told me in an interview (in 2017, not nine years earlier), "When I listen to business owners, they need employees. They need them now." As I write in May 2018, the U.S. unemployment rate is 3.9 percent, which is commonly considered full employment.

As for education data, as reported by the National Center for Education Statistics:

- The percentage of undergraduate credentials awarded in "sub-baccalaureate occupational education" grew from 39 to 42 percent between 2003 and 2011, but then fell back to 38 percent from 2011 to 2015.
- The share of such credentials awarded by public institutions decreased between 2003 and 2011, while the share awarded by for-profit institutions grew. The trend, however, reversed after 2011, as the share awarded by public institutions increased but decreased among for-profit institutions. This pattern coincided with the rising number of closures among for-profit schools starting in 2011.
- Between 2003 and 2015, the number of sub-baccalaureate credentials rose in 10 of 13 occupational fields examined by NCES. Decreases, seemingly

surprisingly, came in marketing, business support, and computer and information sciences.[16]

Can these trends be read as suggesting that for all the attention in recent years regarding non-four-year degrees that great waves of young people have *not* pursued them? That's correct and we'll return to similar data in the conclusion.

For further enrollment context, the Lumina Foundation, in 2018, reported that 46.9 percent of Americans, ages 25 to 64, held a postsecondary credential. This was a significant and impressive (as well as hard to imagine) increase of nine percentage points since 2008. Broken down, a certificate was the highest credential earned by 5.2 percent of Americans in that age range. It was 9.0 percent for associate's degrees; 20.7 percent for bachelor's degrees; and 11.9 percent for graduate or professional degrees.[17]

The core job of America's armed forces is keeping the nation safe. But in doing so they routinely also are excellent places for young people to learn job skills that translate superbly to civilian careers. Google and learn that "the Army offers training in more than 150 career paths" and as an "active duty Soldier, you will have access to all of them."

Then there are community and technical colleges again, but in this instance in their role of helping men and women who already hold four-year degrees, perhaps mostly in the liberal arts, to acquire more marketable skills in their second (or third or fourth) stabs at remunerative postsecondary education. Think information technology or culinary arts, for examples.

And as stepping-stones, there are high school–based programs going by names such as career and technical education (CTE) and school-to-careers (STC), building on or substituting for what used to be more narrowly and eventually pejoratively known as vocational education.

A big reason for the demise of old-school vocational tracks has been the nation's emphasis, going back to the 1983 *Nation at Risk* report and before, on strengthening academic achievement in K–12. But another cause was how vocational tracks frequently led proverbially "nowhere," sending "a lot of kids—especially low-income and minority—into low-paying, menial jobs or worse."[18]

The book's major focus is on what goes on *after* high school. But unless students do reasonably well while *in* high school, they may never graduate from one, much less enroll in any kind of postsecondary program. Especially in this light, the best thing I've read, in preparing to write this book, about better serving kids sometimes described as constituting the "bottom half," is a Harvard report that correctly recognizes that "other countries manage to equip a much larger fraction of their young people with occupationally relevant skills and credentials by their early 20s." And that "lessons from

Europe strongly suggest that well-developed, high-quality vocational education programs provide excellent pathways for many young people to enter the adult work force."[19]

Education reformers praise "continuums of learning" and "smooth transitions" between different levels of schooling, and that's one of the things we're talking about here: the importance of increasing the odds that students leaving high school are adequately prepared to perform well at the next stages of education, wherever and whenever they might be. And that postsecondary institutions aid rather than stymie movement from one institution or system to another.

Back to college. The Brookings Institution reported in 2014 that while "college may be 50 percent more expensive now [in inflation-adjusted dollars] than it was 30 years ago, the increase in lifetime earnings that a college degree brings is 75 percent higher. In short, the cost of college is growing, but the financial benefits of college—and by extension, the cost of *not* going to college—are growing even faster." (Emphasis supplied.)

The vital point to keep in mind, and it's central to the book's argument, is that these numbers are averages that mask the fact that significant numbers of people who hold one-year and two-year credentials and degrees make more money than those who hold four-year as well as graduate degrees. Or, as I recently heard it put, excellent plumbers tend to make more money than mediocre middle managers and bureaucrats. Moreover, chapter 4 will cite perhaps emerging return-on-investment studies that document how men and women with less-than-four-year degrees often earn more money than men and women with baccalaureates, in large measure because of smaller student debt loads and lower opportunity costs.

Yet over and above, making modestly more money in a job that doesn't excite would seem to be ultimately less satisfying for most people than making fewer bucks in a job that does, in fact, cause a man or woman to look forward to getting out of bed at 6 a.m. This is the case even if such latter jobs are commonly considered less prestigious.

A fundamental matter that is pursued less frequently than one might imagine is the origins and nature of the view that "just about everyone" should aim for a four-year degree. This assertion is certainly in the cultural air, even though—the point is particularly rich—I've known only one person, as noted above, to ever explicitly say it. This was a half century ago when a radical political scientist told me exactly that, albeit stopping short of adding anything like, "Unmotivated students of America, DON'T unite!"

So, if few if any people really believe that virtually everyone should seek a B.A., why is the idea, or something akin, as powerful as it is?

In talking to large numbers of groups and individuals about this book and the Center of the American Experiment project that gave it birth, Great Jobs

Without a Four-Year Degree, I routinely begin, as I did a few minutes ago, by noting there are many young people who deep down don't want to attend a four-year institution but do so because of various parental, peer, and other pressures. Within seconds, significant numbers of heads are bobbing up and down in agreement. It's as if virtually *everyone* knows it's absurd to expect such large proportions of high school students to seek a bachelor's degree—even though such potent expectations are, in fact, "out there," both shaping and misshaping the educational and life plans of vast numbers of students.

As for origins, the significant degree to which soldiers returning from World War II made use of the G.I. Bill signaled the birth of mass higher education and its enrollment explosions. This was followed by the even larger degree to which baby boomers born between 1946 and 1964 enrolled, and then to an even greater degree by subsequent generations.

College enrollments in the United States in 1939–1940 totaled a rounded-off 1.5 million students.

The number rose to 2.4 million in 1949–1950.
Followed by 3.6 million in 1959–1960.
Followed by 8.0 million in 1969–1970.
Followed by 11.6 million in 1979–1980.
Followed by 13.5 million in 1989–1990.

Jumping ahead a quarter century, the number of students enrolled in American colleges and universities in 2014 was 20.2 million men and (mostly) women.[20]

A subsequent update showed 20.4 million students were expected to attend American colleges and universities in the fall of 2017, about 7 million of whom would attend two-year institutions and 13.4 million of whom would attend four-year institutions. Of that total, approximately 17.5 million were expected to enroll in undergraduate programs and 3 million in "postbaccalaureate" programs.[21] All numbers include community college enrollments.

Overall college enrollments actually have decreased since early in the 2010s—according to one calculation, by about 1.2 million students between 2010 and 2016.[22] Though it needs noting that this decrease in enrollment coincided with a dip in the population of 18- to 24-year-old men and women in the United States at about the same time.[23]

Again, a major takeaway from all of this is that despite the complimentary things I and others say about associate's degrees and certificates throughout the rest of the book, young and reasonably young people, for whom such options and programs are mainly intended, have not been as enthusiastic in the main. It's lukewarm news to be contended with. Having said that, college enrollments and the state of the economy often move inversely with each other. Meaning, once jobs became more plentiful after the Great Recession a decade ago, many people moved from taking classes to taking jobs.

Speaking of the original iteration of the G.I. Bill (referred to occasionally by its formal name, the "Servicemen's Readjustment Act of 1944"), I've routinely cited it as the effective kickoff of the "everybody" in college movement. But the exceptional and prolific education scholar Chester E. "Checker" Finn saw matters differently by upwards of two generations when I interviewed him. While agreeing that policies such as the G.I. Bill "opened up" colleges and universities to much broader swaths of students—think similarly, he said, of the University of California system, which enabled all comers to attend at least a community college—he argued that it has only been in the last decade-plus that notions that nearly everybody *should* go to college took hold.

As evidence he pointed to "well-intentioned, mobility-minded, good liberals, starting about 10 years ago or maybe earlier, perpetuating the proposition, with a lot of support from big funders like the Gates Foundation, that everybody should go to college. That was typical of what right-thinking liberals and a fair number of conservatives were saying, and it gave birth to an entire mindset."

I worked for Checker in the U.S. Department of Education 30-plus years ago. I've never made it a practice to disagree with him in print, not that I've had much reason to do so. But we're not exactly on the same page or decade this time around, as my preferred start date for the energetic urging of even more people, albeit not "all," to enroll in college was 1968 and the upheaved aftermath of Martin Luther King's assassination that year. Then, again, in another interview, a second old friend and colleague, Ivan Charner, who has worked for decades in the broad area of school-to-work policies and practices, agreed more with Checker than me. Settling matters, I trust our disagreements are mostly of definition and consequent timing.

An important reason I refer to Dr. King's assassination is that I was a student at the time, as noted, at what is now Binghamton University, when total campus enrollment, if I recall correctly, was about 2,700 undergraduate and graduate students. Of that number, I don't believe more than a dozen were African Americans, which is to say they represented far less than one percent of the student body.

Manifestly, the times were such that it rapidly became impossible, both politically and morally, for immense enrollment disparities like that to persist at a public university in New York of all places, and Binghamton enrollment numbers changed quickly and measurably. I would suggest that similarly irresistible demands for expanded access and justice began playing out immediately in colleges and universities all throughout the nation. Those calls may not have been for "everyone" to matriculate, but they certainly were for many more African Americans and other people of color than had been the case.

As for the fact that increasing proportions of teenagers, regardless of race, began envisioning four-year degrees for themselves, I would point to two additional dynamics, one mainly in the province of students and the other of parents.

In 1997, Kenneth Gray, a professor of education, reported that "Ninety-five percent of high school sophomores surveyed in a recent [U.S.] Department of Education study said they would go directly to college after high school, and 85 percent aspired to at least a four-year degree."[24]

In 2011, sociologist James E. Rosenbaum wrote that a remarkable (or not so remarkable) 80 percent of "low-achieving seniors who plan a degree" have an 80 percent failure rate.[25]

And in 2014, a British sociologist, John Jerrim, reinforced Rosenbaum's finding when he wrote that "American teenagers are less realistic about their prospects of obtaining a bachelor's degree than young people in most other developed countries."[26]

How have parents chipped in? Despite findings like those by Gray, Rosenbaum, and Jerrim, as well as the fact that only somewhat more than a third of Americans eventually earn a bachelor's degree, 92 percent of parents in a 2010 Gallup poll said their own children would, in fact, go to college. Given artificially high expectations of this magnitude on the part of Mom and/or Dad, it's hard not to imagine great proportions of young people harboring unrealistically high expectations, too.

In terms of business success and broader prosperity, what about the impact of too few young people mastering the kinds of technical skills commonly acquired via apprenticeships, community colleges, and the military? Suffice it to say the effects of such educational failure are deleteriously large. Pick a trade or industry and then Google it with the word "shortage" attached, and you'll get lengthy headlines and subheads such as: "Construction Boom Exposes Labor Shortage: The Housing Upturn Has Strained a Greying, Shrinking Pool of Skilled Tradesmen, with Few Young Laborers Ready to Pick Up the Slack."[27] Or up will pop articles in which a group of CEOs speculate about what could go wrong with the economy.

Yet after acknowledging potential disasters such as the "Chinese debt bomb finally exploding," the author writes, "What we've really been chewing is what's already a problem: the shortage of skilled, manufacturing labor required to replace retiring workers and allow for growth over the next decade."[28]

It's not as if business groups and industries as well as many education institutions aren't working overtime to train and recruit more people. One of the things I've learned is that more efforts are under way than people in general, and students and parents more particularly, assume, with not nearly enough young people taking advantage of widespread opportunities. This is the case, in part, because what might be described as an overarching and compelling narrative has been missing. One of the aims of *Education Roads Less Traveled* is constructing such a frame and story line, in part by spotlighting success-friendly stories.

For all the pluses of students seeking alternatives to four-year degrees there are several routinely unacknowledged problems and downplayed concerns to be alert to. As teased, one reason for the decline of career and vocational education, or more precisely, a politically and ethically saturated cause of its erosion, is riveted in matters of class and race.

It's hard to see, for example, how suggestions that greater numbers of students forgo four-year degrees will not be interpreted by many skeptics as "tracking redux." American education has a history of keeping disproportionate numbers of low-income and African American high school students out of academic tracks, often for no reason other than their class and race, shunting them to vocational and commercial ones instead. Required now are assurances that what we currently have in mind has nothing to do with what was discriminatorily true then. Or, as a particularly insightful interviewee put it, the "respectability" of certain types of education "has to be restored before you can recommend it to people whose biggest challenge is lack of respect."

Further complicating matters is the fact that the kinds of alternative educational paths advocated here generally will prove most helpful and attractive not to kids from affluent families but to kids from poor and lower-middle-class ones. This makes it imperative for proponents of alternative paths to stay miles away from dissuading, or trying to dissuade, anyone from seeking a B.A. if that is his or her dream and plan. Much better simply to say "Congratulations" and "Godspeed."

Another personal aside: I come from one of those lower-middle-class families, in fact from the archetype of such places: Queens, New York. I've already mentioned what an irresponsible teenage student I was and that coming out of high school I couldn't even get into a community college. But given what I'm urging many to consider, and in the interest of full disclosure, I had no intention whatsoever back then of pursuing anything other than a four-year degree, no matter how crooked a route it required. This was the case not just because I had few, if any, mechanical or manual talents, but as I allowed above, I romanticized about colleges and universities, even to the point of envisioning elbow patches on my tweed jackets.

However, and obviously, the kinds of technical paths that wouldn't work for me more than 50 years ago are conducive for very sizable proportions of Americans currently. This includes those who may start off in tentative quests of a B.A. or B.S., but who learn before long that more satisfying and shorter educational routes are wide open to them. To the extent any of this is interpretable as my proposing for others what I presumptuously had no intention of pondering for myself, my apologies.

Back to "concerns to be alert to." An issue related to the class-rooted and race-rooted reasons for the decline of vocational education is the sense that teachers and principals, particularly in inner-city schools, are increasingly calling their students "scholars," attaching college pennants to nearly every available wall, and explicitly making the case that everyone should envision themselves in college someday. Obviously, this is not the most supportive classroom and schoolhouse environment for talking up the virtues of educational programs that lead to blue-collar jobs.

And a third concern. Increasingly over the decades, college-educated men and women have tended to associate with other college-educated men and women. By "associate" the reference here is largely to marriage, but not exclusively. Will marital possibilities become fewer if the proportion of people choosing non-four-year routes increases, causing those with more education to be less interested in them? Might educational and occupational pathways advocated here paradoxically further depress marriage rates and deepen social stratification? Or dwelling on bright sides, might they lead to more intermarriages across classes and modes of dress and uniforms?

A fourth concern. A particularly insightful friend, in talking about educational options other than a four-year degree, pointed out the expanded extent to which young people likely would have even less exposure to the liberal arts. A fair point, which got me countering that no one is preventing anyone from ordering Great Books and other books on Amazon. But this is a decent rejoinder only if people, in fact, place orders for books and then actually read them, with neither event likely to occur in adequately sizable numbers. But stepping back, how much serious reading and studying do disengaged students on the precipice of dropping out of high school or college usually do in the first place? On average, not much.

Methodologically, *Education Roads Less Traveled* is in large measure the product of 1,000 pages of double-spaced transcripts, composed of 37 recorded interviews, involving 56 men and women from a variety of backgrounds. The book is also significantly the product of library research, though the main library visited this time goes by the name of Google. And it's the product of a wide range of things my Center of the American Experiment colleagues and I have been thinking, writing, and speaking about over the last two years as part of our Great Jobs Without a Four-Year Degree project. As for the thousand pages of transcripts, as sobering as that number sounds, it's still below the 1,400 pages for each of two previous books of mine. Proudly or not, it looks like I got off relatively easy this time.

As for the interviews, which also included an additional two dozen nonrecorded sessions with other leaders, this is the fifth book or dissertation in which I've used this approach: conducting lots of interviews either with one or multiple respondents on any single occasion, and then immersing myself in mounds of paper for a year or more in search of themes, paradoxes, insights, agreements, disagreements, and otherwise interesting observations and arguments.

It's not an approach I would recommend to anyone for whom drowning in reams of data is not a conceivable option. But for some idiosyncratic reason it's a method that came naturally to me, starting with my dissertation more than 38 years ago (only about 830 pages that time), and I evidently do it reasonably well, or perhaps I just don't know any better. I am overjoyed to report, though, that the invention of the "Find" feature on computers has made things blessedly easier than was the case when typewriters were as high-tech as I got, and a bottle of "Wite-Out" was the forerunner of the "Delete" key.

For reasons of finances mostly, all but five of the 56 recorded interviewees are Minnesotans, with the other five from Texas, Maryland, and Washington, DC, which is where their sessions were held. Is this concentration of people from one state ideal? No, but the group is diverse in assorted occupational, educational, political, and other ways; not just racially, ethnically, or in terms of gender.

More than 20 are women. About 20 are current or recent high school or college students (often with big loans). About 10 are racial minorities. About 10 are educators. And about 10 are businessmen and businesswomen, with other interviewees generally working in government and nonprofits. (These numbers total more than 56 because of overlaps.)

If we were to add the approximately two dozen people whose conversations were not recorded to the 56 whose conversations were, I knew about 35 of the more than 80 men and women beforehand, with others generally recommended by a variety of people, ranging in age from teens through Social Security recipients.

As for what we all talked about, this is the fifth time I've used a variation on what sociologist John Lofland described as "intensive interviewing with an interview guide."[29] Or what I describe as "going with the flow of semistructured interviews bordering on conversations."

In the matter of Google and occasionally Bing, it once again has been fascinating that after a couple of early trips to the library for this project, generally all that was needed was tapping a few more keys. I'm not entirely comfortable with this, as writing a book without taking up residence in a library doesn't seem right. But because one of the things this book celebrates is technologically powered new ways of working, I guess I should accept this miraculously effective and efficient one gratefully.

The rest of the book is in seven chapters. Here's a preview.

Chapter 2. How does the idea that just about *everyone* should go to college, which is usually defined as attending nothing less than a four-year school, persist as a North Star when it's universally understood to be absurdly unrealistic and unwise? How can one explain the origins and power of an idea no one takes literally? What role has the G.I. Bill played in setting the norm? What about parental, peer, and teacher pressures? Or severe limitations of high school counseling? Or the fact that people with bachelor's degrees make more money, albeit always on average, than men and women without them?

Or how have perpetual efforts aimed at making K–12 academically stronger and more accountable ever since the release of the *Nation at Risk* report in 1983 drained shop classes and other types of vocational and career education of financial support and the allegiance of educators and politicians? To what extent is mass higher education conceived in some quarters in hyper-egalitarian terms, meaning that anything less than encouraging virtually everybody to go is unacceptably elitist? Or, as one interviewee put matters visually, "When was the last time you saw a football or basketball game on television with community colleges?"

Chapter 3. Exactly what are the good jobs that don't require a four-year degree but can lead to solid middle-class careers and lives? Drawing on multiple sources, the chapter cites dozens of occupations, starting alphabetically with air ambulance paramedics; aircraft mechanics; artisans who hand-craft high-end furniture; auto technicians; builders of complex gas turbine generators; cardiovascular technologists; cement masons; computer support specialists; and, in honor of Jacques Pépin, chefs. Plus, perennials such as carpenters, electricians, and plumbers.

What are the educational routes for getting jobs like these, as well as many others such as glaziers; heating and air-conditioning specialists; installers of cutting-edge robotic assembly machines; ironworkers; and the increasingly celebrated job of welder? Cited in the chapter and throughout the book are two-year associate of arts (A.A.) and associate of applied science (A.A.S.) degrees, one-year and two-year certificates, apprenticeships in different fields, and job training in different arms of the military.

Also described are a surprisingly large number of training programs across the country collaboratively led by leaders in business, education, government, and trade unions. Also discussed are constant pleas that a better job be done of educating students and parents about interesting and well-paying non-four-year opportunities and doing so earlier in young people's lives.

Chapter 4. Avoiding major college debt, seemingly an increasingly compelling goal of many students and their parents, is one of the spurs behind the book's interest in advocating career routes other than four-year degrees, as trying to pay back loans is a crippling deal for many young men and women. Still, it would be a mistake to assume that students with the biggest debts regularly wind up with the nastiest financial troubles. They generally don't, as they tend to graduate from the most respected institutions, win the best-paying jobs, and contend with unemployment less often. According to one scholar, lower-income students who take unfocused courses at community colleges, and then don't graduate, are frequently hurt most by college debt, even though what they owe may be comparatively small.

Average college debt across the country hovers around $30,000 per student, which is far from small change. But something is amiss if a person doesn't value their education as much as the price of a modest Ford or Chevy. Yet, what if he or she is interested in seeking a graduate or professional degree and can do so only by taking out additional loans? At that point, what might have been only a moderate burden might no longer be so.

Chapter 5. Economic growth in the United States is already cramped by too few skilled people in the trades, construction, and manufacturing. The problem threatens to grow worse as 10,000 often highly skilled baby boomers hit 65 every day.

According to one report, three-and-a-half million manufacturing jobs "likely" would need to be filled in the decade between 2015 and 2025, but because of skill gaps, two million of them won't be filled at all.

According to another report, the need to strengthen math and science education in high school goes beyond interest in producing scientists and engineers, as the study recognizes that the kinds of jobs available to high school as well and college graduates increasingly demand "at least rudimentary skills in these fields."

And according to a third report, U.S. employers increasingly complain about how young adults are "not equipped with the skills they need to succeed in the 21st century workforce."

If there is reason here not to worry excessively, it's that national reports have been saying things like this for a long time. Nonetheless, in all of this, there is a risk of making too little of what may turn out to be a dreadful problem for many people: a future of automation and artificial intelligence in which they won't fit because of inadequate or wrong skills.

Chapter 6. Two complicating issues addressed in this chapter are particularly intricate. One focuses on matters of *marriage* and class and the other on matters of *race* and class.

In regard to the former, will women with four-year and graduate degrees be as interested in becoming seriously involved with highly skilled and well-paid men in the trades as they are with highly skilled men who have B.A.s and M.B.A.s? Starkly put, will such women be matrimonially uninterested in men who wear uniforms to work instead of suits and ties? Or will significant differences in education backgrounds pose no great problem, as the men we're talking about will have good-paying jobs—and money, as a couple of interviewees put it, talks?

In matters of race, might referring to elementary school boys and girls loftily as "scholars" make parents less receptive to considering technical and alternative education and career paths for their children? Starkly again, might suggestions about working with one's hands be interpreted by many mothers and fathers as echoes of vocational education and its frequently dead-end tracking?

Chapter 7. Yet what is it about working with one's hands that can be so quietly joyful?

Ole Thorstensen is a carpenter in Oslo. "I like my hands: They have been formed by my age and my work. Some scars, none of them large, all the fingers intact, they are my work: carpenter's hands. . . . My history can be read in them, I think: my hands look like what I have done and do in life. They are a testimonial, my personal CV."

Peter Korn is a furniture maker: "It was not just making furniture that I loved, but also *being* a furniture maker. I like being self-employed, working hard to my meet my personal standards, and trusting in the skill and strength of my hands."

I'm good friends with one of the major contractors for U.S. Bank Stadium in Minneapolis where the Minnesota Vikings play, where the 2018 Super Bowl was held, and which was nearing completion as I began working on this book. At breakfast with him around that time I began waxing how thousands of men and women had worked on the stadium and how, for the rest of their lives, they could tell their children and grandchildren with deep satisfaction, perhaps as they drove by together, "I helped build that."

Chapter 8. How much momentum is there propelling the education and career options advocated in the book? Enrollment data say not as much as one might assume or hope. What policy, practice, and cultural fixes might accelerate change? Here's a sampling.

Career and technical education in high schools and junior high schools should be strengthened and expanded.

Accomplishments of high school graduates who seek non-four-year education and career routes should be celebrated as enthusiastically as those of students who aim for elite colleges and universities.

Better advantage needs to be taken of social media in spotlighting the advantages of non-four-year routes to excellent middle-class jobs and careers. Such social marketing, aimed at both students and parents, needs to use multiple platforms and humor.

In addition to focusing on recent high school graduates, four-year and non-four-year routes and careers should be viewed as lifelines to adults who have floundered, perhaps to the point of dropping out of the workforce.

Insofar as high school counselors generally are ill-equipped to provide information and direction about technical jobs and careers, businesses need to fill the breach.

A perhaps surprisingly large number of programs across the country exist in which business, industry, union, education, and other groups collaborate in urging young people to consider careers in the trades. Such programs also train young men and women in necessary skills. Their number and reach should be expanded.

Most fundamentally, and as is the case with all efforts to change the culture, leaders in a variety of fields who believe more students should consider non-four-year postsecondary options should speak up more and write more than they currently are.

NOTES

1. Anthony P. Carnevale, Nicole Smith, and Michelle Melton, *STEM*, Georgetown University Center on Education and the Workforce, October 20, 2011.
2. Aaron M. Renn, "Manufacturing a Comeback," *City Journal*, Spring 2018.
3. Oren Cass, "Not Everyone Should Go to College," *Wall Street Journal*, May 18, 2018.
4. Dee DePass, "Manufacturing Booms, but Labor Runs Dry," (Minneapolis) *Star Tribune*, May 18, 2018.
5. Philip Trostel, *It's Not Just the Money: The Benefits of College Education to Individuals and to Society*, Lumina Foundation, October 13, 2015, p. 3.
6. Mitch Pearlstein, *From Family Collapse to America's Decline: The Educational, Economic, and Social Costs of Family Fragmentation* (Lanham, MD: Rowman & Littlefield, 2011); and Mitch Pearlstein, *Broken Bonds: What Family Fragmentation Means for America's Future* (Lanham, MD: Rowman & Littlefield, 2014).
7. William Julius Wilson, *The Truly Disadvantaged: The Inner City, the Underclass, and Public Policy* (Chicago: The University of Chicago Press, 1990).
8. Mitch Pearlstein, "Maybe Fewer People Should Go to College," (Minneapolis) *Star Tribune*, August 15, 2010.
9. Robert I. Lerman, "Skill Development in Middle Level Occupations: The Role of Apprenticeship Training," IZA Policy Paper No. 61, May 2013, p. 5.
10. Anthony P. Carnevale, Jeff Strohl, and Neil Ridley, *Good Jobs That Pay Without a BA: A State-by-State Analysis*, Georgetown University Center on Education and the Workforce, 2017, p. 1.
11. https://www.trade-schools.net/articles/trade-school-jobs.asp.
12. Nicholas Wyman, *Job U: How to Find Wealth and Success by Developing the Skills Companies Actually Need* (New York: Crown, 2015).
13. "Success in the New Economy," YouTube.
14. Matthew B. Crawford, *Shop Class as Soulcraft: An Inquiry into the Value of Work* (New York: Penguin, 2009). The title is a play on the title of a 1983 George Will book, *Statecraft as Soulcraft: What Government Does*.
15. Lerman, pp. 23–24.
16. http://nces.ed.gov/pubsearch/pubsinfo.asp?pubid=201810.

17. http://strongernation.luminafoundation.org/report/2018/.
18. Ibid.
19. *Pathways to Prosperity: Meeting the Challenge of Preparing Young Americans for the 21st Century*, Harvard Graduate School of Education, February 2011, p. 38.
20. The first six enrollment figures, between 1939 and 1989, are from the "Biennial Survey of Education in the United States," National Center for Education Statistics, released in November 1992. The 2014 figure can be found at https://nces.ed.gov/fastfacts/display.asp?id=98.
21. "Fast Facts," "Back to School Statistics," National Center for Education Statistics. No date.
22. https://statista.com/customercloud/global-consumer-survey. An estimated drop from 21.02 million students in 2010 to 19.84 million students in 2016.
23. "Fast Facts."
24. Kenneth Gray, "The Gatekeepers," *Techniques*, 72(1), January 1997.
25. James E. Rosenbaum, "The Complexities of College for All: Beyond Fairy-Tale Dreams," *Sociology of Education*, 84(2), April 2011, pp. 113–17.
26. John J. Jerrim, "The Unrealistic Education Expectations of High School Pupils: Is America Exceptional?" *The Sociology Quarterly*, 55(1), pp. 196–231.
27. Patrick Sisson, *Curbed*, February 1, 2017.
28. Mary Josephs, "Manufacturing Labor Shortage: How to Make Your Company a Happy Exception," *Forbes*, March 15, 2017.
29. John Lofland et al., *Analyzing Social Settings: A Guide to Qualitative Observation and Analysis*, 4th ed. (Belmont, CA: Wadsworth, 2006).

Chapter 2

The Four-Year-College Bias

I trust it's clear I'm not an overheated critic of American higher education. I don't know how many people, for instance, ever wanted the "Minnesota Rouser," the fight song of the University of Minnesota, played as the recessional at their wedding, but I did. I don't know how many cellphone ringtones blare the Rouser, but mine does. And I assume the number of twentysomethings who have ever had the privilege of working closely with a remarkable university president, benefiting from five years of personal tutorials in the process, is not terribly large, either, but I did in the 1970s.

Thanks in good part to serendipity, I began working with President C. Peter Magrath at what is now Binghamton University in 1972. He had just been named to lead the school at age 39. I was 24. Two years later he was elected president of the University of Minnesota at age 41, and I went with him as his speechwriter. I was 26. I left his employ three years later to return to graduate school full time, finishing three years after that with a Ph.D. in educational administration with an emphasis on higher education.[1]

Right in the middle of that five-year stretch, in 1975, Caroline Bird's high-profile critique of the very institutions that both Peter and I often revered, *The Case Against College*, was released. I didn't think much of it—not that I read much of it at the time. I have come to view American higher education less romantically than I did 40-plus years ago, though I still part company with much of what she said back then, especially the acerbic and mocking tone with which she said it. The same holds true of my attitude toward many current critics. My interest, however, in recalling Bird's argument has less to do with the exaggeratedly bad deal she pictured college being back then and more with how she propelled the idea that there is an overwhelming norm "out there" pounding young people with the message that almost all of them should seek a four-year degree. This, for example, is how she put it in a magazine, also in 1975:

> The premise, which I no longer accept, that college is the best place for *all high school graduates* grew out of a noble American ideal. [Emphasis supplied.] Just as the United States was the first nation to aspire to teach every small child to read and write, so, during the 1950s, we became the first and only great nation to aspire to higher education for all. During the '60s we damned the expense and built great state university systems as fast as we could. And adults—parents, employers, high school counselors—began to push, shove, and cajole youngsters to "get an education."

A key question before going any further: Have you ever heard *anyone* contend that *all* high school graduates should go to college, especially the four-year kind? I didn't think so. I have heard it said once. It was back in those 1960s, when I was an undergraduate, by a radical political scientist. Other than her, no one. So if hardly anyone ever actually says it or believes it, why do so many teenagers feel pressed to seek a four-year degree, even if they really don't want to, believing it not best for them, much less doable, given their interests and talents? The all-purpose answer is that such high-octane spurs come from all sources and directions: parents, peers, teachers, counselors, and media, with the "very air" and culture breathed by young people adding oxygen to the already-powerful mix. We will return to these influences frequently, but let's start with a little pageantry.

Sandra Kresbach is the executive director of the American Technical Education Association. In an interview, she was talking about how most people are unaware of the key role played by technical education in research and development. I asked her to tie that blindness to the country's fixation on four-year degrees, as opposed to other types of postsecondary education. Part of the problem, she said, is that "four-year education has so much pageantry around it. It has all the sports teams, the mascots, and the huge life, while technical education is very focused on what students are learning, on skill sets, on various industries, on jobs. It's very hard for school counselors, for the media, for parents, for others to get a handle on what the lives of students in technical education are like."

I must admit, antediluvian me, that Kresbach's insightful comment got me thinking about how I perceived—or more accurately, dreamed about—American higher education when I first started doing so six decades ago. I envisioned guys wearing elbow-patched tweed jackets and smoking pipes. I imagined them dressed up at fraternity parties along with coifed coeds. And my mind's eye saw the young men—who seemed relatively old—playing football. While I couldn't replay conversations they might be having, I did have a sense that college men enjoyed talking about Great Books and Big Ideas—at least when they weren't talking about Big Games and Big Dances. To the extent remnants of such fantasies survive in anyone, chances are that community colleges are not featured in them.

Where might I have picked up romantic notions like these? In a fascinating article about organizational identity in higher education, David J. Weerts, Gwendolyn H. Freed, and Christopher C. Morphew write, for instance, about how popular media, going back generations, played a defining role in creating the "collegiate ideal" in the United States.[2]

"The national preoccupation with college was initially stoked by colleges themselves, but soon thereafter, college mania was manufactured for mass consumption by people and entities outside of higher education. Madison Avenue copywriters, Hollywood film producers, radio personalities, and New York literary agents were among those painting a picture of college life that was at once glamorous, manly, and madcap." And then, starting in the second half of the nineteenth century, "Campus calendars were filled with events promoting ceremony, pageantry, and large crowds, including newly established Founder's days and Homecoming weekends."

Some of these traditions continue, and, as witness my earliest conception of college, so do reverberations of movies like *The Adventures of Frank Merriwell*, in which a "humble, temperate, yet indomitable Yale athlete . . . solves mysteries and rescues people from harm while keeping up with his studies." College as a robust and classy rite of passage.

I noted in chapter 1 how the G.I. Bill in the aftermath of World War II made it possible for millions of Americans to attend college who otherwise couldn't afford to do so. I also noted how upwards of 85 to 90 percent of high school students say they plan on earning four-year degrees, with similar proportions of parents expecting their children to do exactly that, or at least hoping they will. But also noted in chapter 1 were James E. Rosenbaum's finding that 80 percent of "low-achieving seniors" who plan on getting a four-year degree fail in doing so[3] and John Jerrim's finding that "American teenagers are less realistic about their prospects of obtaining a bachelor's degree than young people in most other developed countries."[4] What other factors might be at play in driving such audacious numbers, be they about high or deflated hopes? Consider the role played by high school counselors.

One of the most frequent themes I've heard in talking to people about this book is that high school counselors—who a college official I interviewed called "overwhelmed" by too much work—rarely advise students to consider educational routes other than a bachelor's degree. They don't talk enough about well-paying and challenging careers made possible by completing one- or two-year certificate programs, apprenticeships in the trades, training in the military, or the like. Jobs, for example, in modern manufacturing, in high-tech health care, or in a wide range of other fields.

A distinguished report coming out of the Harvard Graduate School of Education in 2011 talked about how students, particularly in what has come to be called the "bottom half," faced barriers such as "weak or nonexistent career counseling."[5] But beyond the fact that counselors generally don't know very much about jobs in construction, plumbing, and such, why do they now seem so much more likely to recommend that their students apply to four-year colleges than pursue other avenues to middle-class careers and lives? Or, in the pungent words of a businesswoman I interviewed: "Guidance counselors have no clue whatsoever about manufacturing." Or, as an educator involved with manufacturing put it: "It's kind of a foreign concept for them to talk about technical education."

In a 1996 article, the same James E. Rosenbaum cited above, along with two colleagues, investigated a variation on the question. "Counselors in the 1960s," they wrote, "had authority to influence who applied to college," but their role "had changed in light of past criticisms of their role in channeling" and because of the vast expansion of community colleges.[6] In interviews, the three authors found that guidance counselors "do not like giving students bad news about their future prospects, do not want the responsibility, and do not believe they have the authority to do it, especially when parents have opposing views." Rather, "they advocate college for all and emphasize personal counseling, which allows them to avoid unpleasant realities."

It's a short jump to understanding why most guidance counselors are not particularly interested in urging students to consider careers in fields that might be disparaged as "vocational"; never mind, once again, that most of them don't know much about the trades and similar professions in the first place.

Consistent with this, many high schools, the head of a builders' association said in an interview, "have eliminated their vocational programs so that we're not giving young people opportunities to even consider such fields as careers. Our view is that construction is a pretty attractive industry, and if more people are exposed to it, large numbers will want to stay in it."

Of the notion "college for all," authors of a superb 2011 report wrote, "'College for all' might be the mantra," but the hard reality is otherwise. The United States, it notes, "now has the highest college dropout rate in the industrialized world." It also argues that a "narrowly defined 'college for all' goal—one that does not include a much stronger focus on career-oriented programs that lead to occupational credentials—seems doomed to fail."[7]

Similarly, we learn from another source that only four out of ten Americans have a four-year or two-year degree by their mid-20s.[8] But then we learn from a celebratory Census Bureau news release that in 2011, "for the first time ever, more than 30 percent of U.S. adults 25 and older had at least a bachelor's degree."[9] The choice is yours about whether these proportions reflect a half-full or half-empty vessel.

The word "channeling" above is pivotal, though it's less stark than "tracking," which was what large numbers of counselors and other educators were guilty of when it came to their encouraging, or not encouraging, many low-income and minority young people to attend one kind of educational institution or another, if any kind of postsecondary institution at all. Given how tracking has fallen out of favor, it's easy to see why counselors have come, in effect, to say, "Who needs that aggravation?" "Who needs to be called a racist?" Or, in the matter of female students, "Who needs to be called a sexist?"

For decades now and in great numbers, school counselors and other educators have suggested, both implicitly and explicitly, that vast majorities of 17-year-olds should, in fact, aspire to the academy if that is their stated wish. Or perhaps counselors have simply acquiesced, implicitly or explicitly, in doing so.

Glaringly missing, of course, from the above recitation of reasons why four-year degrees are regularly seen as compelling is how holders of bachelor's degrees generally do better financially than people who don't hold one. Debates are perpetual over the size of college premiums, but for our purposes, a summary by Stephanie Owen and Isabel Sawhill of the Brookings Institution is useful, although it contrasts how much more money four-year graduates make compared to men and women with only high school degrees, instead of comparing men and women with four-year degrees to those with two-year degrees (which we'll do in a moment). Still, it's informative, and a condensed version of their summary might go like this:

"We all know that, on average, college graduates make significantly more money over their lifetimes than those with only a high school education. What gets less attention is the fact that not all college degrees or college graduates are equal. There is enormous variation in the so-called return to education depending on factors such as institution attended, field of study, whether a student graduates, and postgraduation occupation." Owen and Sawhill conclude their synopsis by writing, "For certain schools, majors, occupations, and individuals, college may not be a smart investment. By telling all young people that they should go to college no matter what, we are actually doing some of them a disservice."

As for returns on four-year versus two-year degrees, the "typical" bachelor's degree holder, at least by one calculation, makes about $335,000 more over the course of his or her career than does the "typical" associate's degree holder: approximately $1,190,000 compared to about $855,000.[10]

Without underplaying Owen and Sawhill's last comment about how it can be a disservice to urge people to go to college "no matter what," I would guess the proportion of young people who have believed they would wind up among those for whom a bachelor's degree makes no economic sense has been modest, thus reinforcing the four-year bias. This last sentence is written in the indicative present perfect tense because of increasing numbers of stories and anecdotes about college graduates having hard times paying back their college loans, especially while cornered behind counters at Starbucks. We'll return to this complicating and often dispiriting theme in chapter 4, which addresses the growing role of college debt, accompanied by growing concerns about underemployment. But for now, Checker Finn told me during an interview, "I'm persuaded the wastage of people dropping out of college with no credential, but with debt, is a scandal. It's an outrage, frankly."

Another strut undergirding a four-year bias, which we will return to at greater length in later chapters, is immersed in questions of social justice. The same Prof. David Weerts quoted above is a friend at the University of Minnesota. Seeking his thoughts about the roots of the bias, he pointed out that proposals like mine, showcasing the virtues of alternative educational routes, make many people nervous about social stratification. Whose kids, exactly, will wind up in less-than-four-year programs? Might they be disproportionately of color and low-income? In light, should not nearly all young people be encouraged to seek a baccalaureate? A reflection of this aspiration is the seemingly growing movement of teachers in inner-city schools addressing all their students as "scholars." More about this in chapter 6.

An African American woman said in an interview how she had been firmly told by her family, "You will go to college. You will not be able to achieve what we know you can achieve unless you have a degree." She got one and then a master's, too. Are white women (and men) told the same thing, just as firmly, by their families? Yes: every day. But chances are, any historical baggage accompanying those directives is less heavy.

Back to what interviewees thought about the four-year-college bias, especially since none of them contended it doesn't exist. What do they see as its ramifications? And what do they say might be done to at least soften its edges? Let's start with a story from several years ago involving King Banaian in dual roles as a father and academic. An economist, he is currently dean of the School of Public Affairs at St. Cloud State University in Minnesota.

> When my son Aram graduated from high school, he could go to any of the Minnesota state universities basically tuition free since I worked in one of them. So, I kept asking, "Which one do you intend to go to?" After he chose Moorhead State, one of the seven four-year schools, I asked, "What are you thinking of majoring in?" He said English, since he said he "kind of likes English." I said,

> "Yeah, professor's son. That makes sense." I drove him there but it turned out the part about going to classes was not something that really interested him. Video games were much more appealing than his freshman English class.
>
> At the end of the year, I picked him up, and on the drive back he said (I think these were his exact words): "By mutual agreement, I will not be returning to Moorhead next year." After almost crashing the car and giving him an earful for 15 minutes, which was followed by probably five minutes of silence, I said, "So what do you want to do? What's your plan?" That's when he said, "You know, Dad, I've always wanted to cook." To make a long story short, he lived with us for a year and went to the local technical college. He earned a one-year culinary certificate and has been cooking ever since and is hoping to own his own restaurant.

I asked King if his son, while he was in high school, had ever said, "You know, I really want to go to cooking school."

"No," he said, "because he was afraid what my answer would be."

I asked the dean if he thought his pressure had been implicit. He said "absolutely." I noted that I assumed it also came from peers and other sources, to which King agreed and said high schools likely pressure students to attend four-year schools as it "improves their prestige." Aram had attended the public high school in St. Cloud.

Meet hardware entrepreneur Dave Svobodny, who also attended a technical school, but that was his plan from the start. Dave is the owner of the hardware store I frequented for the 26 years that my wife and I lived in South Minneapolis. I forget exactly what precipitated it, but early in thinking through this book, we had an enthusiastic sidewalk conversation about how he started in the business, which led to my interviewing him several months later. He is now in his early 50s. I asked how he had come to choose what he described as a "trade school" after finishing high school.

"I wanted to make sure I was going to get a job, and at that time cable TV was getting very, very strong. I wanted to go to school to be a cable TV technician."

The cable program, however, at the technical school he wanted to attend was full. He enrolled, anyway, thinking he'd be at the front of the line when a spot opened. To get matters rolling, he was still required to pick a program, which he assumed would be only temporary. How did he do that?

"This is totally a true story," he assured me. "The brochure containing course listings for Dakota County VoTech opened up like an old-fashioned road map. I didn't really care what I picked, since it was my second choice, so I covered my eyes, dropped my finger, and it landed on 'hardware management.' I did some investigating and found out you don't make much money in hardware to start, but you could end up being a manager, or a sales rep, or a store owner and do all right. I said, 'Well, okay, I'll try this and I'll keep my eye on the cable program.'"

Dave wound up completing and thriving in his "second choice" program as he quickly discovered he loved everything about hardware and hardware stores, as witness the fact that he now owns three of them and is doing financially quite nicely. But I wanted to know if his high school friends who overwhelmingly attended four-year colleges while he was attending a two-year institution had given him a hard time. Yes, they had, but mostly in joking and good-natured ways.

The clear sense one gets in talking to him is that he was not bothered in the least by the kidding, even when it accelerated around women he might be interested in, as he firmly knew what he wanted to do. The fact, moreover, that his parents supported his decision to bypass a four-year school reinforced his strength. His father, not incidentally, was a teacher. "Trade school for me," Dave said, "was awesome. For the first five or six years, nobody wanted to walk in my shoes, but after they saw everything start to blossom, they were going 'Holy Smokes.'"

I thought of strong backbones again when I interviewed two young men who had chosen to attend two-year schools after graduating from a Christian academy. Regarding the four-year bias, one of them said, "I just kind of bulldozed my way through it, and it was fine." His friend added that he had "definitely felt the pressure, but it wasn't prevalent enough to be an influence in my life."

Another interviewee, a business owner, told of a graduating high school senior, a friend of one of his sons, who said when asked what he was going to do: "'I really want to be a mechanic, and I really want to work on big Caterpillars.' And he got real excited about it." The interviewee then said, "And his mom is like, 'Yeah! And we're proud of him too.' This is a big thing."

As pleasing as this kid's comment was about being a mechanic, there might have been more complexity to it than suggested here in two quick sentences, as he immediately proceeded to "look down at his shoes."

Maybe the young man was just shy. Maybe his shoes were Air Jordans and he was admiring them. Or maybe there was a part of him uncomfortable about announcing he was going after a credential other than a B.A. Though one would hope he's the kind of guy, as described to me by an interviewee, who's truly excited about working on and playing with huge pieces of equipment. That interviewee, a pipefitter, spoke of how much he loved doing his thing atop immense cranes, not that he was a particularly young man anymore. As for the broader point, at a breakfast meeting with a group of educators and others, a college president talked about how "we've got to move technical education to a better place."

Without building up any of this too high, think for a moment about the kind of fortitude exhibited by the two Christian academy graduates. It's one thing for a kid to ignore a near cultural mandate if he is a bad student and wants no part of four more years of school. Similarly, if his grades and test scores are such that he has few viable four-year options. Or, if he just wants to do something else at that often wander-lusting stage of life, like joining the military or taking a gap year in exotic places, as one young woman I interviewed did. But it's quite another thing for an excellent or reasonably decent student to resist doing what most peers and parents see as an educational imperative.

More precisely, it's noteworthy when good students stand up to a force that most of their parents not only believe in but deeply *feel*. Think of the self-confidence it might take for 17-year-olds to declare, proudly, they're going to a local community college or trade school when almost all their friends are announcing their Ivy and other four-year acceptances.

Then, again, perhaps more unavoidably than heroically, many students wind up in two-year schools not because they want to be there, but because neither they nor their parents have enough money for a four-year one. Or, wisely, because they are determined to keep college debts as small as possible.

But then there was another mother who was talking to a college administrator about her son, a high school junior, and his interest in robotics. This news was met enthusiastically by the official, who offered to arrange for the boy to spend a whole day with a professor at a nearby community and technical college, at which point the mom said her son would never go to the school in question, as he automatically dismissed it as a place for "druggies and losers."

The administrator told me his wife later said it "looked like I had been sucker punched." The dismissal by the high school student, the administrator said, "was the spoken version of the kind of thinking a lot of people harbor. They generally don't say it, but they harbor the impression that technical education is less-than."

To this, Rassoul Dastmozd, president of a two-year institution, Saint Paul College, might say (as he said to me): "We need to get rid of the perception that a two-year technical college or a comprehensive community college is a place where your child, who supposedly can't make it anywhere, can land. I am appalled when I talk to a parent saying, 'Well, my daughter Stephanie is gonna go to XYZ college, which is very competitive, Big Ten, Big Twelve, private, whatever. But my son Johnny is a little slow. I think you ought to do something with him.'"

As if on cue, Minnesota's commissioner of higher education, Larry Pogemiller, told me a few weeks later, "I would hope I would have the courage to say to one of my daughters, 'Sweetheart, you really don't need to go to the University of St. Thomas, or wherever you're thinking about going, as Saint Paul College will be great, because here's what you want to do.'"

Or, as Dastmozd said, "We take everybody. This is a place for everybody under the sun. We just have to figure out what their goals are. We need to get away from this whole notion of labeling institutions that provide technical training and demeaning them, saying that, 'Well, if there is no place for her over there, she can always land back here.' Why don't we start here and move her to the next trajectory, is the way I look at it."

Perhaps not incidentally, *Washington Monthly*, in both 2010 and 2013, named Saint Paul College the top community college in the nation. Agreed, rankings like this by popular publications should not be taken too seriously. Then, again, the detailed tour of the place that Dastmozd gave me was more than a little impressive.

A public affairs executive told me this during an interview: "My cousin became a welder, but first he had to get a four-year degree because his parents pushed him through it. From the start, he had wanted to make his living welding and finally did so when he finished his B.A. He's a great welder. He loves to sculpt. He loves to do all kinds of welding. But he also wants to know, 'How can I go back so I don't have more than $100,000 in debt? Why wouldn't my parents look at trade schools as great places for me to go? Why couldn't I live my trade to begin with?'"

Another person, a woman in her 20s who researches and writes about public policy, reported on four-year degrees and romance:

"When my parents first found out we were seriously dating, the first question out of my dad's mouth was, 'Does he have a four-year degree?'"

To which I said, "You're kidding? Exactly that?"

"Yes," she said, "exactly that. I guess his reason for saying it first is his belief that men with less formal education are less financially stable, so he was concerned we would enter a marriage where the man couldn't be the man, the head of the household. And with that could come financial insecurity, when money in general is the number-one thing married couples fight about, or so I've been told."

I assume her fiancé, who has a two-year degree and is a cybersecurity expert, will do just fine professionally.

An aside: As I was writing this section, someone asked if my two oldest grandchildren, both high schoolers, would be going to college. No doubt the person doing the asking was thinking of four-year institutions. In less than a second I automatically blurted, "Oh God, yes," or something like that. Another sign of the bias instinctively at work.

And then there was a mother, Amanda Norman, a religious woman, who I'm sure would be accepting, perhaps even joyously so, if one or more of her children chose a path other than a four-year degree (though her oldest child already attends an Ivy). I had just asked her how her faith colors everything we had been talking about.

"I do feel my children have a vocation because of their relationship with their creator. God has given them talents, characteristics that He wants in this world. As a parent, I need to steward those talents—whatever they may be."

I asked how she was using the word "vocation."

"A calling," she said, "a purpose."

The "exotic gap year" teased earlier, which covered a good portion of the planet from Southeast Asia to Central America, was taken by a young woman who had just graduated from a prestigious private high school in the Twin Cities and who is now attending a strong liberal arts college. "I felt stuck in a system where there was a lot of pressure to take all these extracurricular activities just to keep my options open for college."

Her decision to take a year off, she reported, left her college counselor not especially pleased. "I told her I didn't have cold feet about college and felt ready to go. But at the same time, this was more of where my heart was. As I moved on with the process by myself and with my family, she eventually came around and supported my decision."

In another roundtable, I asked several other young women if they had classmates who hadn't wanted to go straight from high school to college. "I think if you grilled them," one said, you would find "they hadn't even thought about not going to college. It was so ingrained in their minds that it's not even a consideration." But if you *really* drilled down, she added, "I bet there would be people who would say, 'You know, I'm not really excited about going right away.'"

Another impressive high school student I interviewed, albeit one from radically different circumstances, was a young man born in a refugee camp in Thailand, who was now a senior at a typically diverse public high school in Saint Paul and who planned on making his career in the trades. His family was from Burma. I asked Lah Htoo if anyone was pressuring him to seek a four-year degree instead.

"Not lately, no. Most of my friends are going to get their four-year degrees, and I'm one of the only guys who has a backup plan. If my first plan fails, then I can go to a second, and if that fails, I can go to a third. I've applied to Century College [a two-year school in a Saint Paul suburb]. I'll go there and then switch to a university. That way, it's a lot cheaper. So if I find out during my time at a two-year school that college isn't for me, I won't have a huge debt and stuff."

I asked if he viewed himself as an outsider.

"Somewhat, yeah. My friends think that you can't make a good living without a four-year degree, but I have a different opinion about that. There are plenty of jobs out there. You can get some kind of certificate and get a good job."

I asked where he learned about certificates.

"I did my research. The first thing I know is I like working with my hands. But people with four-year degrees usually work in a cubicle." After referring to various jobs in the trades, he finished off the thought by saying, "You can get your welding certificate."

"Welding," the prototypical and seemingly most frequently mentioned job that doesn't require a B.A. or B.S., strikes again.

At one point, someone else in the room asked Lah if he ever felt unwelcomed on jobsites because he's "not a white kid." It was good to hear him report, "I don't feel unwelcome in any way. Because of the unions, everyone are brothers and sisters. They treat each other like family, and they work together to get a job done. It doesn't matter if your race is different or your gender is different."

The "someone else in the room" was one of Lah's teachers, Roy Magnuson, a well-known and respected veteran teacher and coach in Saint Paul. He made several important comments during that session, and I interviewed him alone a short time later. Given that he had long worked in the vineyards of what I was now more or less writing about, I opened the latter conversation by asking, "What should I know?"

"There's a lot everyone should know," starting, he said, with how "the four-year college path has become not just the 'preferred' path, but almost the only path. This is the case at local, state, and national levels. Part of it is the result of conscious policy. Part of it is the result of the never-ending quest for accountability regarding public money. It's easier to look at how many kids graduate, how many go to college, what their test scores were, how they did on college-track classes, and the like."

Five days earlier, when I interviewed Lah Htoo, Magnuson put matters this way: "The pressure was intense to make everything pre-college, and some of us thought this was a mistake and spoke up against it. But we were accused of believing some kids can't succeed. There were accusations thrown about that we didn't believe certain groups could succeed. It was unpleasant."

I asked if the pressure to attend a four-year school was as "real" for low-income as for higher-income students. "I think they are," Magnuson answered. "In fact, I don't just *think* they're real. I *know* they are."

NOTES

1. C. Peter Magrath, now a barely slowed-down 85, was one of the more than 80 people I interviewed for this book.

2. David J. Weerts, Gwendolyn H. Freed, and Christopher C. Morphew, "Organizational Identity in Higher Education: Conceptual and Empirical Perspectives," in M. B. Paulsen (ed.), *Higher Education: Handbook of Theory and Research*, Volume 29 (Dordrecht: Springer Science + Business Media, 2014).

3. James E. Rosenbaum, "The Complexities of College for All: Beyond Fairy-Tale Dreams," *Sage Journals*, first published March 22, 2011.

4. John Jerrim, "The Unrealistic Educational Expectations of High School Pupils: Is America Exceptional?" *Sociological Quarterly*, 55 (2014), pp. 196–231.

5. *Pathways to Prosperity: Meeting the Challenge of Preparing Young Americans for the 21st Century*, Harvard Graduate School of Education, February 2011, p. 13.

6. James E. Rosenbaum, Shazia Rafiullah Miller, and Melinda Scott Krei, "Gatekeeping in an Era of More Open Gates: High School Counselors' Views of Their Influence on Students' College Plans," *American Journal of Education*, 104 (August 1996).

7. *Pathways to Prosperity*, pp. 7–10.

8. Nancy Hoffman, *Schooling in the Workplace: How Six of the World's Best Vocational Education Systems Prepare Young People for Jobs and Life* (Cambridge, MA: Harvard Education Press, 2011), p. 1.

9. "Bachelor's Degree Attainment Tops 30 Percent for the First Time," News Release, Census Bureau Reports, February 23, 2012.

10. Brad Hershbein and Melissa S. Kearney, "Major Decisions: What Graduates Earn Over Their Lifetimes," *Hamilton Project*, September 29, 2014. Hershbein and Kearney's analysis draws on the Census Bureau's American Community Survey.

Chapter 3

Underemployed Paths to Great Jobs

OK. What are all these great jobs that don't require a four-year degree but can nonetheless lead to solid, middle-class careers? And how to win them? We've mentioned some, but if we were to pull together a much fuller list, what would it contain, over and above welding, which both Sen. Marco Rubio and I, for some reason, tend to cite first? As noted in chapter 1, recall how Senator Rubio, in a presidential primary debate in 2015, asserted "We need more welders and less philosophers." Given that he said "less" where he should have said "fewer," I wrote back then what we really needed were more English majors, but I pedantically digress.

I also frequently mention trades such as carpentry and plumbing, plus several other jobs such as X-ray technician and massage therapist. But what other occupations (1) generally don't call for a four-year degree; (2) yet still require postsecondary training of some kind; and (3) usually pay reasonably well? The following eclectic albeit incomplete roster, in awkward alphabetical order, is drawn from various publications, especially *Job U: How to Find Wealth and Success by Developing the Skills Companies Actually Need* by Nicholas Wyman[1]; "Skill Development in Middle Level Occupations: The Role of Apprenticeship Training," by Robert I. Lerman (2013)[2]; and a governmental document or two.

> Air ambulance paramedics; aircraft mechanics; artisans who handcraft high-end furniture; auto technicians; builders of complex gas turbine generators; carpenters; cardiovascular technologists; cement masons and concrete finishers; computer support specialists; chefs; correctional officers; decorators; dental hygienists; electricians; entrepreneurs who run their own photography studios; firefighters; fitness trainers; and flight attendants.
>
> Glaziers; heating and air-conditioning specialists; installers of cutting-edge robotic assembly machines; ironworkers; law enforcement officers; machinists;

> massage therapists; mechatronics engineers (I had to look it up too); medical records and health information technicians; operating engineers and other construction equipment operators; paralegals and legal assistants; painters; and people who build our homes and bridges.
>
> People who keep advanced manufacturing humming by programming and operating computer-controlled tools and robots; people who keep complex IT networks running; people who monitor our health and care for our sick; people who repair engines; pipefitters; plumbers; radiologic technologists and technicians; salespeople; sheet metal workers; some kinds of nurses; steamfitters; truck drivers; truck mechanics and diesel engine specialists; tuckpointers; veterinary technologists and technicians—and back to welders.

What possible themes might tie all these "A" to "W" occupations together in some fashion? One framing is that I increasingly find myself impressed by people who clearly know what they are doing, regardless of what their jobs or pursuits may be. I'm mightily impressed, for instance, by color commentators who see things during televised sporting events that I don't see. Same with musicians who stop every few seconds during rehearsals to discuss subtleties in what they just played that I don't hear. Or more in keeping with jobs listed right above, I am increasingly impressed, year by year, by the skills of paramedics who save lives, mechanics who keep aircraft airworthy, electricians who turn lights back on, tradesmen who fix things right the first time, and just about everyone Mike Rowe works with on television's *Dirty Jobs* (admittedly a bad title for the point I'm making).

According to the previously mentioned Professor Lerman, an economist and perhaps the nation's leading authority on apprenticeships, while the proportion of what's called "middle-skill jobs" such as those noted above, indeed, have fallen modestly in recent decades, they still comprise nearly half of all U.S. employment. Which is to say, there is plenty of hospitable terrain to explore and profitably mine by people with less than a four-year degree, as long as they continue their education beyond high school in a conscientious way, such as by pursuing a one-year or two-year certificate program in a community or technical college, by taking advantage of excellent job training available in the armed forces, or by doing an apprenticeship. In other words, educational and occupational pathways that are sometimes called "alternative," but, if my reading is correct, that increasingly will be viewed as mainstream.

According to the U.S. Department of Labor, there were 533,000 apprentices in registered apprenticeship programs across the country in 2017. This was a substantial increase from about 375,000 in 2013.[3] The United States is not Switzerland, and Switzerland is not the United States, but in contrast, 70 percent of all students in Switzerland choose apprenticeships.[4]

An expensive homegrown aside: As I was writing this book, my wife Diane and I moved, after 25 years, from Minneapolis to Eden Prairie, a southwestern suburb. Early on, I needed to hire a painter to do a modest amount of inside work to get our Minneapolis house ready for sale. But after a half-dozen calls, I couldn't find one who could squeeze us in for at least three weeks, which would be too long. I finally tracked down a painter by speaking to a friend, who urged me to call a friend, who knew a very good one who might be able to start in a couple of days, which happily he could and did. That time-consuming exercise got me thinking about how dependent we might be on people in the trades and other areas, especially since I'm not the most adept or enthusiastic person when it comes to home repairs. (Having grown up in Queens, it was understood the Yellow Pages were proof of God's existence.) As it turned out, my wife and I were dependent on dozens of men and women.

The following alphabetical recitation contains the kinds of practitioners and businesses we have paid trying to repair and/or jazz up our homes. It may not be a complete listing, as I likely repressed some. I can only guess what kind of education or training each person has, or what kind of credentials they hold, or how much money they make. In other words, I don't know how many ever pursued any of the educational routes I advocate. But I thought it would be interesting to get a sense of all the jobs and fields involved in selling one house and buying another and to note all the possibly well-paid players who might or might not have a four-year degree.

> Appliance technicians, appraisers, boiler technicians, concrete specialists, consignment store owners, electricians, floor cleaners, garage door specialists, and glass specialists.
>
> Handymen, hardwater specialists, hardwood specialists, home inspectors, inside house cleaners, landscape specialists, lighting specialists, mortgage bankers, and moving companies.
>
> Outside house cleaners, painters, plumbers, PODS people, Public Storage people, Realtors, rubbish haulers, security system technicians, stagers, videographers, and window cleaners—but admittedly, no welders.

Given all that moving from one home to another can entail and cost, unless getting out of town is a near-life-or-death imperative, I've taken to urging friends to consider staying put forever.

Let's start digging deeper with a question a semiretired professor friend of mine likes to ask his graduate students in public policy: "How many of you have ever been on a modern factory floor?" Unsurprisingly, few if any hands ever go up. A pipefitter told me that a big reason parents don't want their children ever to work in a factory is that they don't want them coming home greasy every night, when it fact, as he said, they probably wouldn't, as up-to-date manufacturing is more antiseptic than Dickensian.

In related spirit, I wonder every Labor Day how many commentators who write or speak about the holiday have ever made their living using their hands for anything other than typing (like me). And if they are on the young side, I wonder about the immediate environs in which they grew up: How many came of age in working-class neighborhoods? Relatively few, I suspect. How many of their parents wore white collars, just as their well-educated children were destined to wear? Large numbers, I would guess. My sense is that fewer words are written about Labor Day every year, not necessarily because of any political or ideological reasons, but because the number of journalists and other opinion leaders who are familiar with the kinds of work first honored on the first Monday of September is declining year by year.

Or, as put by Mike McGee, a senior official of the Minnesota State College and University System: "Our country did its best in the 1980s and early 1990s to shed our manufacturing and technical base of employment when we believed we'd be offshoring the vast bulk of manufacturing. We were going to do that for a couple of reasons, including how we thought it would be cost effective. But we also sent the message that manufacturing, or that kind of labor, was beneath us."

Mike figures we're still 10 or 15 years away from overcoming that mistake. As for workers who will make that possible, he intriguingly but I trust correctly argued, "I don't think it's any easier to start a two-year program in electrical work, or HVAC, or machine tool technology than it is to start a four-year liberal arts degree." I agree. Mike McGee is the same university official who was told by a mother last chapter that her son wouldn't attend one of his two-year institutions because it was loaded with "druggies and losers."

Speaking of comparative ease and difficulty, one interviewee, Lindsay Benjamin, a program manager with degrees and other credentials from the likes of Carnegie Mellon, Stony Brook, and Harvard, spoke of his longtime dream (more than a fantasy) of changing careers and becoming a professional long-haul truck driver, crisscrossing the country on no fewer than 18 wheels, and sharing the driving and shotgun-riding with his also highly educated wife Darlynn.

"We were talking about this again last week," he said. "We would need to be trained, but in terms of understanding all the different systems, oh, I could envision that right away," which is not surprising, given his professional and other talents. Still, he recognized the physical demands of such a career switch and how one almost "needs to be an athlete" to pull it off. In a subsequent conversation, he said this last reference had more to do with airline pilots than athletes given the "complex dashboard layouts of modern-day rigs and the high level of technical and cognitive proficiency required."

Of the industry, he spoke of how it's short tens of thousands of drivers. One might ask what it is about this well-paying career that's not enticing greater numbers of younger men and women to pursue it by enrolling in training programs in many community colleges and other places. Might it be the job's many physical, cerebral, and other demands, including routine stretches away from families? No question, as it often can be a trying way to make a living. Yet might another obstacle be what some see as the greater allure of middle-management jobs made possible by four-year degrees and nothing shorter? In a magnificent nation of open roads and land stretched by sky, and with all due respect to middle managers everywhere, let's hope not.

How to get more young people intrigued by well-paying careers—not necessarily in factories and plants, no matter how greaseless they might be, but in one of the many other fields already cited that do not require a four-year degree? How to get more parents comfortable with the idea that such jobs are worthy of their sons and daughters? And how to help larger numbers of moms, dads, and teenagers better appreciate that the "smartest and quickest route to a wide variety of occupations *for the majority of young people in the successful countries* . . . is a vocational program that integrates work and learning?"[5] (Italics in the original.) While our focus is on what young people wind up doing after high school, it's essential to know something about what's available, or not available, to them beforehand. Given the subject at hand, this is particularly the case when it comes to technologically enriched curricula going by embellished names such as career and technical education (CTE) and vocational education and training (VET), not merely "vocational education" anymore.

Whatever happened to plain-old voc ed? In severely rough and truncated terms, it suffered from (1) the 1983 *Nation at Risk* report which argued that students needed to take more academic courses lest a "foreign power" possibly have its way with us; (2) subsequent "reforms," especially the drive for standards, accountability, and testing; and (3) a "college for all" mentality discussed last chapter. All of this deepened a stigma long associated by many with vocational courses and tracks.

Think of CTE as a countervailing effort to lessen that stigma by enriching curricular offerings by "integrat[ing] traditional academic subjects with technical, job-specific skills"[6] and in the process making such programs more attractive and welcoming, particularly to the significant portion of young people—very much including kids from solid middle-class families—whose interests and talents are more technical and hands-on than traditionally bookish.

A 2016 study[7] of Arkansas high school students who took CTE courses encouragingly found:

- Students with greater exposure to CTE are more likely to graduate from high school, enroll in a two-year college, be employed, and earn higher wages.
- Students taking more CTE classes are just as likely to pursue a four-year degree as their peers.
- CTE provides the greatest boost to the kids who need it most—boys—and students from low-income families.

In complementary spirit, a former Teach for America teacher is of the mind that CTE helps students develop the "non-cognitive abilities that all children need—grit and self-control, leadership, and interpersonal communication skills."[8]

I was skeptical about the Arkansas results at first, but they are more credible once it's understood that large majorities of high school students across the country take at least one course classified as a CTE offering at some point; it's not as if only small subsets of often academically aloof young people do so. The Association for Career and Technical Education, in fact, reports that CTE "encompasses 94 percent of high school students,"[9] though their definition of "encompasses" is rather expansive.

Gen Olson, who turned 80 a week before I wrote this page and who is theoretically retired, was a longtime vocational education teacher and administrator in Minnesota, with a doctorate in the field. She also was a longtime Minnesota state legislator, and when Republicans held the majority in the chamber, she was chair of the Senate Education Committee. One of her legislative successes was making it possible for tenth-grade students to take a career and technical education course at a postsecondary institution as part of Minnesota's Postsecondary Enrollment Options program, and if they received a C or better, they could take more courses. PSEO had previously been limited to eleventh and twelfth graders.

In our conversation, I asked Gen to make connections among her interests in vocational education with her doctoral work and what she wound up doing in the legislature. Three excerpts:

"I constantly saw how education's academic side was viewed as superior to the vocational side and just as constantly tried to figure out how to get past that. I just saw that some people learn better in an applied way. We pay lip service to individual differences and styles of learning, yet we've done very little about that. We put students through the same mold."

"There was a professor at the University of Minnesota in trade and industrial education by the name of Mel Johnson. He had done a study of high school students in a vocational program compared to students in a strictly academic program regarding how they did in math. He found that students in courses such as machine trades did better on basic math tests than those who had come up the academic route."

"Mel likewise told me about a group of high school teachers, who taught academic courses, touring an Area Vocational Technical Institute in Mankato when one of the teachers stopped to watch a student work at a precision machine. As everyone else moved on, she stayed and watched. Finally, the student asked, 'Is there something I can help you with?' I don't know how long the woman had taught, but she told him that was the first time she had ever seen one of the mathematical principles she taught actually being used."

Without getting into the weeds concerning name changes and governance changes, AVTIs were the forerunners of Minnesota's technical colleges.

Roy Magnuson, whom we met last chapter, is a veteran teacher at a Saint Paul high school which has yet to get into any full-fledged CTE or VET swing. But his commitment and respect for his students, great numbers of whom are low-income and minority, are manifest. One of the things he spoke about in our several meetings and interviews was how "we have taken opportunities away from many kids, both male and female, to showcase what they can do. We've always had kids who have found what's left of our wood shop to be a place of creativity." But as witness his reference to "what's left of our wood shop," that is less the case now. "One of the things I try to do every year is go to the education building at the State Fair, as it still has things that kids make in shop classes and where they can win blue, red, and white ribbons. It's important for them to enter, compete, and win something. It's important that we help all kids feel like they can do good things."

Mitch Davis, a large-dairy owner and another one of our interviewees, was of similar mind when he said, "We would be better served if we found out what kids love, what young people love, what they really have a passion for, and guide them to those areas, whatever the tracks may be." His comment followed a discussion in which he spoke of how a majority of high school graduates who have sought jobs at his business couldn't do eighth-grade math—a required skill level for running mixing equipment at the dairy.

A perpetual theme in interviews was the need to inform students, as well as their parents, earlier in their school careers than is now the case about interesting and well-paying, non-four-year opportunities—if, in fact, informing students and parents about such things is now done at all. Some said efforts should be made when high school students are freshmen and sophomores. Others recommended when boys and girls are in junior high school. And at least one interviewee, Rassoul Dastmozd, president of Saint Paul College, an exceptionally well-respected two-year school in Minnesota's capital, said "before fifth grade." "We need to expose the youth of this country to the opportunities available to them at the very earliest stage, before even fifth grade. You already see it in affluent elementary schools where kids attend coding camps, scrubs camps, and the like."

Myron Moser is principal owner of multistate Hartfiel Automation, whose formal education ended with his graduation from a two-year technical school. Or, as he puts it, "My education has been primarily self-inflicted." "Educating kids," he said, "about the kinds of jobs that are possible without a four-year degree has to be done in junior high school, because by the time they get to high school, the die is kind of cast. Those expectations are reinforced by their families, and once that happens, it's pretty tough to change."

Darlene Miller is owner of a precision manufacturing business. The "We" she refers to is a nationwide, editorial one: "We haven't worked enough with high schools and middle schools, which is where we really need to start. Think if you were in Germany: Kids there know by middle school about different paths. Kids here aren't exposed to them, and it is businesses that have to educate and excite them."

Incidentally or not, President Dastmozd graduated from a German high school.

Related or not, Roy Magnuson said it was "concerning" that students were being asked "earlier and earlier to commit to making life decisions" without "letting them live a little longer." A fair point, although I trust he agrees that learning about career options and committing to one of them are not the same thing.

Which brings us to the role played—or, more frequently, not played—by high school counselors. (Also referred to here as "school" counselors and "guidance" counselors.) Recall that we discussed last chapter about how they (1) are overwhelmed by enormous caseloads; (2) usually know little about jobs in manufacturing, construction, the trades, and various technical fields; and (3) recommend that just about everyone seek a four-year degree if students have an inkling of doing so, because school counselors would rather not be thought of as biased racially or in any other way. The interviewees I met with recognize that counselors' own educational backgrounds are grounded in four-year degrees and master's programs, not technical subjects, with their professional lives routinely played out much more within the walls of school buildings than outside them. And where their days are more regularly consumed trying to help troubled teenagers deal not with career plans but with a gamut of emotionally taxing problems. Here is a brief collage of interviewee comments:

- "Guidance counselors really don't do career counseling. They don't really talk about what students can do after high school. But they're glad to help with college applications."

- "We have guidance counselors doing everything. They're being family members, they're being advocates, they're being mental health counselors. They're not providing academic planning because of all their other priorities."
- "Talking about technical education is a foreign concept for most guidance counselors. They need to recognize that its expectations on students are on a par with demanding curricula in four-year schools."
- "We have totally inefficient and ineffective college and career counseling, starting in middle school and going through postsecondary. There's a lot of career information out there, but kids don't get it. Counselors deal with student ratios of 600 to one and 700 to one and handle socio-emotional issues. And then they get rewarded for the Ivy League schools their students go to."

Given their caseloads, a case certainly can be made that hiring more counselors would not be spendthrifty. But if the aim is providing students with more and better information about non-four-year routes to good jobs, hiring more men and women with the same lack of familiarity with such career paths would be wasteful and futile. In light, my interviews and conversations frequently turned to how business leaders might more effectively connect with high school students and sometimes younger kids. Most discussions like these, however, were immediately punctured by mutual recognition that teacher unions would not stand for any arrangement in which they saw their interests and members, plausibly or not, undermined in any way.

But what if business officials, and not just in human resources, could go about their own brand of career counseling, not in school buildings, but in nearby offices or community centers? Or even more conveniently, in trailers and other logo-emblazoned vehicles parked outside schools? I raised ideas like this with a foundation president who liked them but already had been told "no-go" by local teacher union leaders when she raised them herself.

None of this is to say businesses, business associations, schools, and school districts can't jointly pursue educational and training-training projects for the benefit of all concerned, as the nation is increasingly rich in such endeavors. My Center of the American Experiment colleagues Katherine Kersten and Catrin Thorman have focused on several of them, as when Kathy wrote about the Central Minnesota Manufacturing Association (CMMA), which aims to expose high school students to manufacturing as a career.

"We were having trouble," one of the group's leaders said, "attracting young workers," as parents "would discourage kids—telling them modern manufacturing is 'dark, dirty, dangerous,'" and that all manufacturing jobs had gone to China, anyway. In the works when Kersten wrote about CMMA, in 2017, was a major project to help businesses in the "complex business" of hiring high school juniors and seniors as apprentices.[10]

In Washington State, a National Public Radio story spoke of how parents "want something better" for their sons and daughter, other than jobs where they would come home "dirty" every night, which is not to say they necessarily would.[11] The excellent story, which focused on a training program for ironworkers near the Seattle-Tacoma International Airport, noted how participants were cleaning up, making $50,000 and $60,000 a year while still in the program. One participant spoke of his old high school friends who were still in college: "Someday maybe they'll make as much as me." The report noted he said this with a "wry grin."

Back in Greater Minnesota, Kersten wrote about Wright Technical Center, a consortium of eight school districts operating a program called Creating Entrepreneurial Opportunities, or CEO. Working with mentors, high school students tour local businesses and meet with owners to learn what it's like to start and run a business. Kersten quotes the project's coordinator as saying, "Every week, after we tour a business and sit down with the owner, I hear the same thing from students: They say, 'I've driven by that building my whole life and I never knew what they do there—I didn't know they make parts for the Space Shuttle, or medical devices, or whatever.'"

And Kersten has written about how, in West Virginia, students are benefiting from a "new-and-improved approach to CTE" in which officials hope to prepare high school students for highly skilled work in the fracking industry, presumably among other fields.

One of the more innovative initiatives I've learned about is a program called Tennessee Promise.[12] According to Michael Krause, the executive director of the Tennessee Higher Education Commission, in 2012, Gov. Bill Haslam asked (in Krause's words), "Could we change how students think about their own future? Could we change how they think about what college means?" And that was the genesis of the Tennessee Promise. The program affords high school graduates a chance to attend one of the state's technical colleges for free.

I'm generally not a fan of free tuition once students get beyond high school. This is the case for budgetary reasons and because many people will succumb to the temptation of not working hard since they have little financial skin in the game, as the cliché goes. But what I like about the passage above are the questions posed by Governor Haslam about helping students improve how they think about their future, reinforced by his spurring them to think anew about what college means.

As noted by Kevin Smith, Nissan's North America manager of technical training, Tennessee Colleges of Applied Technology needed more space while Nissan needed to conduct more programmable logic controller training.

The company, likewise, needed more space. So, according to Smith, Nissan made an offer it hoped the state couldn't refuse: It would provide the land if Tennessee would build a facility, which both sides could share for their mutual benefit.

He said one of the things Nissan wanted to do in the new building "was to be able to bring in middle schoolers, high schoolers, their parents, their teachers, their counselors. We wanted them to see these are good careers. It's amazing to see the parents' eyes open up when you can tell them their son or daughter can go 18 months to [an] industrial electrical mechanical mechatronics program, that's free . . . and come out and make $50,000 to $60,000 a year." And with 100 percent placement at the program's close.

There are far more than enough other germane programs out there to fill more pages and chapters regarding their origins, intentions, successes, and sometimes disappointments. And I will get back to describing several more (victorious) ones and alternative educational pathways in a second, both in the United States and Europe, as well as in chapter 5. But recall in chapter 1 when I wrote that business groups and industries, along with many schools and colleges, have been working overtime trying to attract and educate more people about many excellent opportunities, not that enough parents have been paying adequate attention, or that enough students have been taking sufficient advantage of them.

What has been missing, I argued, has been an "overarching narrative." What might be thought of as a crisper and more compelling story leading to greater recognition that huge numbers of young Americans are poorly served by America's baccalaureate bias and that the economy is not well served by it either. Drawing such a picture and vision is one of the aims of the book.

Back to impressive programs on both sides of the Atlantic and Pacific.

Right Skills Now for Manufacturing is another program that is successfully preparing young, or not-so-young people, for careers in high-skilled manufacturing. Perhaps most responsible for its success has been the previously mentioned Darlene Miller, owner of Permac Industries, a precision manufacturing company in Minnesota, who's also one of our interviewees. "Right Skills Now," she described in our conversation, "was developed when I was co-chair of the high-tech education committee on President Obama's Council for Jobs and Competitiveness. With the help of Dunwoody College and the Precision Manufacturing Association, we developed a fast-tracking training program that involves eight weeks in classrooms and then four weeks of internships."

Permac hires many participants and offers tuition reimbursement programs for students seeking the Right Skills Now program and/or two-year programs at Dunwoody, South Central College, and Saint Paul College. At last count,

Right Skills Now is in 13 states. Dunwoody is a superb and demanding technology college in Minneapolis, about which we'll hear more later.

Nancy Hoffman is a vice president and senior adviser at Jobs for the Future in Massachusetts. She is also author of *Schooling in the Workplace: How Six of the World's Best Vocational Educational Systems Prepare Young People for Jobs and Life.*[13] Remember how, in the previous chapter, Dave Svobodny wound up majoring in hardware management—and making a great career of it—by closing his eyes and blindly poking his finger at a list of courses? That's basically how I learned that in Australia, "VET [Vocational Education and Training] is the country's comprehensive workforce development strategy available to Australians between the ages of 15 and 64": I just closed my eyes and poked at the book's rich index. Same with learning that the Netherlands "provides both subsidies and tax deductions for VET companies—a more complex system than Norway's but worth the scrutiny of U.S. states or regions interested in engaging employers in workplace training." Just closed my eyes and dropped a finger again.

More purposely this time, I was drawn to a paragraph in which Hoffman argues that apprenticeships and sustained internships are "especially effective in meeting the developmental needs of young people," as they "provide a structure to support the transition from adolescence to adulthood, now lacking for the majority of young people in the United States who do not go to residential four-year colleges." Apprenticeships, moreover, "provide increasingly demanding responsibilities and challenges in an intergenerational work setting that lends structure to each day." This kind of home base is not to be underestimated, as there is substantial research showing that college students tend to benefit both academically and socially by living on campus rather than commuting from home.[14]

In an additional useful service, Hoffman neatly distinguishes "certificates" from "certifications" from "licenses" in the United States.[15] Here are abbreviations:

- Educational institutions award "certificates" to indicate completion of a program of study that does not culminate in a "degree." Criteria vary widely among institutions—even within the same higher education system or state.
- "Certifications" are closer to "qualifications" than are "certificates" in that they are awarded by a third party, often a professional organization. A standard-setting entity assesses the applicant's competence against standards in a particular occupational area.
- "Licenses" are the credential most similar to "qualifications" in that they serve as the sole ticket of admission to an occupation; one cannot practice without one. Earning a license to practice usually requires examination

> by a licensing board of experienced practitioners in the same field. It frequently requires that the applicant complete a prescribed course of study and present a certificate or degree attesting to the successful completion of that program.

One increasingly hears of "two-plus-two programs." They apply both to programs which, in various ways, connect the last two years of high school and the first two years of postsecondary work as well as to initiatives in which graduates of two-year institutions, after a spell, enroll in four-year institutions to enhance their careers with a B.A. or B.S. This route often involves men and women with technical jobs who hope to move into management. "What we should do," suggested an interviewee, "is roll many more people going into two-year postsecondary programs with the idea they'll do a two-plus-two sequence. From there, they'll go on to a four-year degree because it might give them the skills to become a supervisor, manager, director, vice president, president, owner, or entrepreneur. Give people a ladder so they can climb it to their potential."

Elsewhere in the book, I note that people who already have baccalaureates but are unable to find good jobs enroll in either two-year or shorter community college programs to, finally, acquire more marketable skills. I've never heard them described as "four-plus-two" or "four-plus-one" programs, but that doesn't mean we can't start now.

Let's close this portion with thoughts about the three other, non-four-year options mentioned several times but not yet adequately discussed: one-year and two-year certificate programs, associate's degrees, and job training in the armed forces.

Beyond the fact that formal apprenticeships are simply not embedded in our country's DNA, and beyond a bias on behalf of four-year degrees that frequently extends to the lowest socioeconomic rungs, why do we do so poorly, comparatively and absolutely, when it comes to apprenticeships? Explanations include how apprenticeships can be too expensive for employers' tastes, as well as their distaste for expanded regulatory obligations and union entanglements.

One builder I spoke to, for example, supports job shows in which representatives of both contractors and unions staff booths pitching young people on career possibilities in the industry. But he's not happy the sessions are dominated by unions (which, in fairness, might have something to do with unions picking up most of the tab for the events). And he's equally unhappy that the trades make it clear "they don't want to work with the non-union side of the construction field."

A conversation, however, I had a year earlier with a carpenters' union leader had a less-combative flavor, as he clearly recognized that builders and carpenters are more dependent on each other, for example, than governmental agencies and public-sector unions are with each other. In the latter instance, workers generally get paid if tax revenues fall; in the former, tradesmen don't get paid if builders are not building. As for Professor Lerman, he added (probably a bit glibly) that if companies want to do apprenticeships largely free of regulations, there's nothing stopping them from going it alone, "as we haven't copyrighted the term 'apprenticeship.'"

In the matter of certificate programs, Sandra Kresbach, whom we met in chapter 2, spoke of using them not just to kick off a long-term career but also as safety nets if the pursuit of a B.A. or B.S. either ends prematurely or doesn't lead to a good job after graduation, with bills nevertheless arriving regularly every month—which might well include making good on loans accrued while at a four-year school. As noted in chapter 1, one-year and two-year certificates can lead to decent-paying jobs as cosmetologists, massage therapists, and certified inspectors of various kinds, as well as to a growing number of computer-related fields, perhaps especially cybersecurity. Think of them here not only as careers but also as backup plans. Or, as put by Matthew Crawford, the motorcycle repair shop owner with a doctorate in political philosophy, "Even if you go to college, learn a trade in the summers."

For a corresponding sampling of jobs for which men and women with an associate of arts or (more usually) an associate of applied science degree qualify, a 2014 study by the Bureau of Labor Statistics found these five to be among the best paid: air traffic controller; radiation therapist; MRI technologist; dental hygienist; and computer programmer, once again.[16]

Fred Senn is a founding partner of Fallon, one of the country's truly imaginative advertising agencies. ("We believe that creativity is the last legal means to an unfair advantage.") He also was one of the more strategic people I interviewed for the book, as when he suggested that if it were up to him, he would advertise the military "as a step between high school and college." In large part this was the product of his own experience during the Vietnam era. "I was Army, but I worked for the Air Force running a missile site in Germany. It was a tremendous educational experience in terms of management, technology, and leadership."

We had been talking a few minutes earlier about working with one's hands, or as he put it, the "art of hard craftwork and how joyful it is." And from there: "There's another need that 18- to 22-year-olds have, and that is community. That's why they go to gangs. That's why they go to small colleges. I don't know if it fits here, but the military gives you a skill set and a community during those very formative years."

A 2007 article by an economist with the Bureau of Labor Statistics reinforced how the "military trains you to be technically proficient in whatever occupation you are assigned," and how you will "learn teamwork, perseverance, leadership and other skills widely applicable in the civilian workforce." The author also noted how military jobs have "direct civilian counterparts.[17]

Senn learned one other thing from his time in Europe: "I saw how apprenticeship programs did wonderful things in building stature in the young people who came to work. They worked alongside people who had been in the crafts for a long time and who treated the kids with respect. We have interns here, but we're not as good with them as the Germans are with their apprenticeship programs."

Having further sketched educational and occupational options available to young people not seeking four-year degrees, let's return to ways of informing them and their parents about such routes. "Social marketing" was suggested many times as a way of doing so more effectively, with the term conceived in both electronic and other ways. Ivan Charner, whom we met in chapter 1 and whose career has focused on collaborations and transitions between school and work, spoke vigorously about failing to take adequate advantage of social media. He also was as critical as anyone regarding the state of in-school career counseling. Here he combines the two streams.

"We don't have social marketing campaigns," Ivan said, "about what's going on, about what jobs are available, about how people can get those jobs, about whether it's through certificate programs, or industry programs, or two-year colleges, or four-year colleges. We have totally inefficient and ineffective college and career counseling, starting in middle school and continuing throughout postsecondary."

Mike McGee, the system director for education-industry partnerships for the Minnesota State University system, is a man of no less passion. He's also the unidentified administrator we met earlier. He speaks here of better educating students and parents about educational and career possibilities by more explicitly informing them about manufacturing:

> If we could only get parents, I mean mainstream city and suburban parents, to better understand the skilled and high-tech nature of career and technical education and the jobs we do. The goods produced and the systems installed and maintained. We'd have better appreciation for technical education. I was in a classroom talking about manufacturing and held up my phone. I asked, "Where do these come from?" Someone said the phone store, and I said, "Before that?" Someone else said China, and I said, "Before that, too." You would have thought I had asked, "How many miles to Mars?" There was stone silence in the room.
>
> I said raw materials, but what I really wanted to talk about was that everything we touch is manufactured. It was built. It didn't just *become*. Someone builds these things. The computers in your hands are among the most sophisticated things humans have ever developed. They're the result of engineering, and obviously there's a lot of four-year and postgraduate work in them. A lot of Nobel

> Prize work in them. But when you get right down to it, the people who make these systems work, who maintain them, and allow us to produce these goods are primarily at the technician level.

The recently cited Lindsay Benjamin, a senior systems analyst, reinforced this point when he spoke of the need, not for computer scientists, but "technologists who actually know how to operate our various systems." Another interviewee, King Banaian, the dean of public affairs at St. Cloud State University, said that one of the reasons two-year programs work is that, by the time a person is impatient, they're almost done.

I next asked Mike McGee what we need to do to persuade more young people and their parents that there are ways to have good lives without four-year degrees. "We need to take advantage of applied experience. Applied learning is powerful. The images. The sounds. The chance to see and touch and operate. To see raw materials going in and finished products coming out. Tours, job-shadowing, informational interviews, and internships. Maybe apprenticeships later, but certainly internships while students are still in high school, whether over summers or released time during the school year. Work-based learning is the Holy Grail of getting folks oriented to careers they had no idea existed."

Another good way of convincing young people and their parents that non-four-year speedways to well-paying and satisfying careers exist, in the construction industry in this instance, is to have them push a few keys to a website sponsored by Project Build Minnesota.[18] This is its opening language: "Today more than ever, America needs men and women who will build. The current labor shortage in the building trades is projected to grow, which means those who join the trades will be paid more, receive more benefits, and enjoy better lifestyles than at any other time in history. While your friends flip themselves upside down with school debt pursuing the next shiny digital trend, you'll begin your career debt free. A career that's in high demand, promising growth, and job security. One that will support a family and make you a better person in every aspect of life. It's your future . . . what do you want to be?"

I'm well past the age of the site's target audience, but I must admit particularly enjoying the line about friends flipping themselves upside down because of school debt.

A bit later a more societally compelling message: "We are the designers, creators, and builders of the world, providing shelter and comfort for our communities and environment. We are the hands that craft and the diverse minds that create. We come together from various backgrounds as the skilled professionals of the industry that work beside each other as a team, ensuring the job is done right. We believe in making a better future for ourselves and our state."

And then a short time after that, the site features an illustrated presentation of 24 different trades and jobs in the construction industry, from A for architect to W (needless to say) for welder. As I write, no evaluation of its effectiveness has been conducted yet, though my senior eyes are impressed.

More mundanely but still essential for getting in front of students and sometimes their parents are school visits, job fairs, career days, Rotary Clubs, Kiwanis Clubs, and the conventional like. Snappier than mundane, I've seen YouTube cartoons effectively making the case that more jobs will continue being available for people with certificates and two-year degrees than people with four-year degrees. As well as a great many more jobs, certainly, for men and women with certificates and two-year degrees than people with graduate degrees.[19]

The overall aim here is exposing students and their parents to a larger number of educational and career possibilities than they likely imagined. One might say the goal is *simply* exposing students and parents to such options, but "simply" does not accurately describe much when it comes to enlarging perspectives in directions we've been discussing. One reason, of course, is the very strength of America's four-year bias. Another is all-purpose bureaucratic. And another is classified as hard to fathom, as what's so hard about getting words and ideas like these out there? But what if both two-year and four-year routes were packaged in more aspirational-friendly and family-friendly ways?

Scott Peterson directs human resources for the Schwan Company. He has thought a lot about questions like these, most recently in playing a central role in the development and operation of Real Time Talent, a business-led private/public collaborative focused on bringing big data and analytics to workforce development, including a fascinating, high-tech means of efficiently and effectively connecting potential employees with potential employers. We had just been talking about a plan proposed earlier by Steven Rosenstone, the recently retired chancellor of Minnesota State, that gladly would give undergraduates a full decade to complete their degrees. "When you come out of high school," Peterson said,

> you may say you're never going to college—that you just want to make 15 bucks an hour so that you can live in a decent apartment, go out on weekends and afford a car. You may be working in a maintenance role in a manufacturing facility and getting some health care benefits. You may even have gotten a certificate of some kind. But then you're 20, and you say, "I may want to be a supervisor someday." So you enroll in a community college and eventually earn a two-year degree, believing that coursework in management will be helpful.

> And it works. You become a supervisor, and at that point you say, "Being a supervisor is all I want to do."
>
> But then, as it routinely happens, you wind up getting married and having a child. And you say, "You know what? I want to do more. I can do more. I'm going to get that four-year degree." But it's going to take you a while, as you now have a couple of kids, and other things may be happening in your life where you don't have extra money, and you realize it's going to take you at least six or seven more years to get a B.A. or B.S. And you wonder if an assortment of university rules and regulations might make it even more difficult for you to get that degree if things stretch out too long or if you and your family move elsewhere.

I challenged Peterson at this point, wondering exactly what rules and regulations would dash academic dreams, as people take a long time to finish degrees all the time. He acknowledged that rules which do exist may cause only frustration and headaches, not stoppage. But we were on the same page when I said colleges and employers need to be more explicitly encouraging and purposeful in smoothing roads, especially when now-older students live complicated lives.

(Shortly after I wrote the paragraph above, my longtime colleague Kent Kaiser, who doubled as the book's initial copy editor, challenged my skepticism that rules and regulations regularly "dash" the academic dreams of people who take a long time to finish undergraduate degrees. A department chair himself at the University of Northwestern–Saint Paul, he noted that seven years is about the limit before new course catalogs replace old ones, and that their numerous curricular changes "can create barriers, as courses passed often become worthless and new courses need to be taken." I stand partially corrected, as I persist in believing most college and university officials are reasonably more flexible than rigid. Professor Kaiser, I know for a fact, is one of the former.)

High schools and employers also came into play when Scott talked about the need for them to better collaborate in informing students and parents, early on, about usually bypassed options. "Parents," he said, "need to attend forums at schools where they can learn that their child doesn't need to accrue $150,000 worth of debt, perhaps like an older sibling, and can still make $40,000 to start. But that there's also a path to a four-year degree and bigger jobs. Just on a different timetable that is more in line with what the high schooler really wants at this time in his or her life, versus what the parent has decided for him or her."

Using his company as the vehicle, and imagining what a high school student might report after attending such a forum, Peterson had the kid saying how he was going to work for the Schwan Company and how they told him of different jobs he might qualify for and how much money he might make.

Plus, how a representative of the company told him, "If down the road, I want to get more education, they will support me. They might even help pay for it." Peterson's argument is that conversations like this are not happening often enough. "High schools are not providing enough platforms for students and parents, and businesses are not aggressive enough in saying that's what they need from schools."

The distinction between higher education and K–12 was purposely blurred when Frank Forsberg, a former United Way vice president, talked about how his father "owned a couple of bakeries at one point in his life. He started as a 15-year-old dishwasher and people taught him the craft." He later went to a trade school to "become more professional in his craft." But it all started because, in his first work experiences, "adults in his environment began to teach him skills as he showed interest, and then he supplemented those efforts. I say this because we have lost those kinds of opportunities, and re-creating them in a way that is efficient and good for students makes sense to me."

One such way, he suggested, and as previously discussed, is dual-credit programs involving both high schools and postsecondary institutions, "Because when I listen to business owners, they need employees, and they need them now! And sometimes when the market changes, they need a different mix of skills quickly. They don't have five years to wait and adjust." It's unclear here if Frank was referring to one educational system, the other, or both. It's likewise open to debate which tends to be nimbler when it comes to jointly accommodating the occupational needs of students and businesses: public school bureaucracies or postsecondary bureaucracies. Thoughts?

We have focused so far on young people in junior high school, senior high school, and older students in postsecondary institutions. But much of what we have said about shaky employment futures also applies to people in their late 20s and early 30s or later still. This is the case especially with men, since they are doing less well than women on virtually every measure one can think of, very much including education.

I visited the Minnesota Carpenters Union training facility in Saint Paul and was impressed. My American Experiment colleague Katherine Kersten also toured the facility on another occasion and wrote about the "many complex skills" carpenters need to master, "such as how to use computerized robotics and GPS to lay out building foundations and how to create negative air pressure environments to work safely in occupied hospitals.[20] Yet the average age of those starting their four-year apprenticeships is 28." The senior union official showing Kersten around said they would "like to get them by age 19, but young people don't seem to see carpentry as a desirable, meaningful career. If they were exposed to its rewards in high school, we could attract them much sooner."

Kersten also spoke to a 27-year-old HVAC technician who didn't start a two-year program at a community and technical college until he was 24, drifting from one job to another before then. He said he would have chosen HVAC a lot earlier if he had known how rewarding and stimulating the work is, but not a single high school teacher ever mentioned the trades as a career possibility.

Demographer Nicholas Eberstadt has written about the enormous numbers of men who are nowhere to be found in the American workforce.[21] Guys who are not just unemployed but missing in growing inaction. There are any number of reasons for this, including opioids and the ability to make do in modern life without doing much of anything, thanks to an array of welfare and disability payments. But clearly, if more men were to get their lives in order by acquiring the kinds of skills we've been talking about, preferably sooner rather than later, more of them would be working, supporting themselves and others.

Factoid: The average American K–12 student spends four hours a day watching television,[22] not to mention other hours in front of other screens. Consider it un-job training.

This is an apt spot to note a story relayed by an interviewee named Marilyn Higgins, who formerly ran a job training program in upstate New York. One of her assignments was helping men and women, though mostly the former, find new jobs after they had been laid off by a major manufacturer. She discovered that many of the men "seemed very capable of either starting their own businesses or getting management jobs that were technical in nature. They didn't need any more technical training, but what they did need was Dale Carnegie, as they were not comfortable in having the kinds of conversations a person needs if they own a business or work as a manager someplace. They weren't confident."

So Higgins put in a request to fund Dale Carnegie courses for them, which was denied, of course, by the public job training agency. "But an anonymous donor said he'd pay for the courses, and we did an experiment. We put 16 men, ages 40 to 45, through the program and they *all* got jobs, almost immediately, with two of them starting their own little businesses that did quite well." The moral of the story, outside of the fact it's a fun one? As Higgins puts it, "There are many jobs out there that don't require a four-year degree and provide platforms for growing wealth." Or, if you will, there's more than one route to activate potential.

Speaking of starting businesses: People in the trades conceive and create their own firms all the time, be they plumbers owning plumbing services, carpenters owning cabinetmaking shops, painters employing other painters rather than being employed by other operations, or construction workers of one kind or another starting their own contractor businesses. And they do so without necessarily having a four-year degree, much less an M.B.A.

One participant in a roundtable discussion, Ted Risdall, spoke of meeting a "couple of folks" in northern Minnesota who were cutting down trees. "Those machines are absolutely amazing. But all these guys are operating their own independent businesses. They're working with million-dollar pieces of equipment and making big money taking these trees down and shredding them for paper, forestry mills, and the rest." Ted is the owner of a large public relations, advertising, digital integrated marketing firm.

Another participant in the same roundtable, Bob Michels, a builder, spoke of a job he was doing in rural Wisconsin. "I got a guy coming out of Rice Lake. His name is Jeff. His email replies consist of 'yes' and 'no.' He's got GPS equipment on huge machines. He's building a 2,500-foot-long and 50-foot-wide road for me, according to specifications provided by an engineer. He's got massive off-road trucks, massive backhoes, millions of dollars' worth of equipment. I'm pretty sure Jeff didn't go to college. He's just a smart fellow who has taken advantage of his knowledge of equipment and probably his passion to operate machinery."

A second pertinent route to becoming an entrepreneur has aspects of apprenticeships, albeit not "official" ones. They are more informal than structured, having to do with mentoring relationships between different-aged friends and relatives, rather than ties between relative strangers originating at worksites. Houston White, who was an interviewee, was fortunate to be the student in several friend-to-friend mentorships, as well as a grandmother-to-grandson one. He attended barber schools in Mississippi and Minnesota. Here's an excerpt of what he said in our conversation:

> I remember going up to "Dimensions in Hair." Mike Spicer owned it, and he's legendary in barbering in Minneapolis. He's the guy who really created the resurgence in barbering in North Minneapolis.[23] I would go to his shop at least once a week, sometimes every day, because I was just fascinated by the environment. He took me outside and showed me around. "Houston," he said, "I figured out late in life what I really wanted to do, and I told myself I never want to work for anybody again because they would control my destiny. And as a black man, you need your own." He then said, "This building, I've got two more years, and it's paid off. Whatever you do, if you get in this field, make sure you own the real estate you occupy. Land ownership is key to your future, your family's future, and your legacy." It was people like that. I have so many stories of folks who poured so much into me.

"H. White Men's Room" has come to be much more than just a barbershop in North Minneapolis, but a vitally engaged community institution in the iconic tradition of African American barbershops. Or, if you prefer, something headier in Houston's words: "H. White's Men's Room is the reinvention of the barbershop providing a range of hair and grooming services in a relaxing environment that caters to an exclusive and sophisticated clientele." Passion at work again.

Let's finish off the chapter with pivotal points about intelligence—or more precisely, perceptions of intelligence—that could have served as the opening but which might have sounded defensive there.

We met industrialist Myron Moser earlier in the chapter. Here's a fuller rendition of his theme:

> Back when I was going to high school, which was a long time ago, the attitude was pretty much the same as it is today: If you were smart, you went to a four-year school. If you were one of the dummies, you went where the rejects went—technical colleges—because they couldn't cut it. Sure, I have a technical college education only, and yet I don't consider myself less educated than many with advanced degrees. I have a great curiosity, and I've gone out and filled the blanks. One year out of tech college, I was building my first brand-new home while my compadres were still going to college racking up debt. But the stigma attached to technical schools hasn't changed.
>
> It's so important to get to parents. I go back to my high school sometimes, and I go to other high schools as an advocate for tech college education. I tell everyone, "I've bought four companies, and I started five more. I've sold one. I've been very successful, very blessed, and I have a tech college education. I have people with advanced degrees who work for me. I think the challenge is that most families, kids, and high schools look at tech college education as lesser. The stigma starts at home, as every family fantasizes about their kid being valedictorian at Harvard or Stanford, right?"

Moser made a compelling pitch for expanding eligibility for Pell Grants to include low-income students "who want a 90-day certificate to be a welder or a carpenter." Current Pell law does not cover programs that short. "Part of the solution to the workforce vacuum," Moser argued, "is bringing in underprivileged communities, but we don't know they're there. They can't afford to press pause and go to college for two years. They're living hand-to-mouth. I chair the effort to provide crisis grants for Hennepin Tech students, and their stories are heartbreaking. Single mothers' cars break down, they lose their jobs, and then can't pay their rent. Things like that. They want to build better lives for themselves and their families, but we need to expand Pell Grants to help them do that."

My conversation with Moser was in January 2018. A month later, it was reported that the "Trump administration's proposed budget allows student borrowers to use Pell Grants for short-term, non-traditional degree programs, such as vocational or technical schools."[24]

Moser spoke of the "stigma" starting at home. My American Experiment colleague Kathy Kersten, in an op-ed titled "Postsecondary Education for Non-Dummies," wrote of a mother "who was in mourning" because her son had chosen to attend a two-year technical college instead of four-year school, and she feared he had "lost his chance at the good life."[25] Instead, Kathy argued, "her son may have made a shrewd decision." Students who "choose alternative pathways—like a two-year associate's degree, an apprenticeship, or an occupational certificate—can often land in-demand, well-paying jobs fast, avoid crippling debt, and look forward to a secure future." And on top of it all, "Some earn significantly more than classmates who choose the four-year route."

Speaking of the increasingly unavoidable matter of college debt, that is where we now turn. Though, as a heads-up, there are arguments to be made that the student debt problem is not as severe as it's often portrayed. Or at the least, it's more complicated, in surprising ways, than it's usually made out to be.

NOTES

1. Nicholas Wyman, *Job U: How to Find Wealth and Success by Developing Skills Companies Actually Need* (New York: Crown, 2015).
2. Robert I. Lerman, "Skill Development in Middle Level Occupations: The Role of Apprenticeship Training," IZA Policy Paper No. 61, May 2013.
3. https://doleta.gov/oa/data_statistics.cfm.
4. "Swiss Apprenticeship Model: An Employer Driven System of Education and Training," Business and Schools in Collaboration (BASIC).
5. Nancy Hoffman, *Schooling in the Workplace: How Six of the World's Best Vocational Education Systems Prepare Young People for Jobs and Life* (Cambridge, MA: Harvard Education Press, 2011), p. 6.
6. Jessica Poiner, "CTE and Non-Cognitive Skills: A Match Made in Heaven?" Thomas B. Fordham Institute, February 16, 2018.
7. Shaun M. Dougherty, "Career and Technical Education in High School: Does It Improve Student Outcomes?" Thomas B. Fordham Institute, April 7, 2016.
8. Poiner.
9. "CTE Today!" Association for Career and Technical Education, January 2018. In a private correspondence, ACTE's Catherine Imperatore wrote: "The 94 percent statistic includes students taking any number of credits in various occupational areas as well as family and consumer sciences and general labor market prep."
10. Further information on CMMA, along with information on the next two projects cited by Kersten, can be found in Katherine A. Kersten and Mitch Pearlstein, *Great Jobs Without a Four-Year Degree: A 2017 Review in 30 Eclectic*

Blogs and Commentaries, Center of the American Experiment, Golden Valley, MN, February 2018.

11. Ashley Gross and Jon Marcus, "High-Paying Jobs Sit Empty, While High School Grads Line Up for University," NPR News, April 25, 2018.

12. The following information about Tennessee Promise as well as collaboration among Tennessee Colleges of Applied Technology is from a 2017 panel discussion in Nashville sponsored by the American Technical Education Association. Quotes have been mildly edited for clarity. "Mechatronics," by the way, is a technology combining electronics and mechanical engineering.

13. Hoffman.

14. Going back a long time now, see for example, A. W. Astin, *Four Critical Years: Effects on Beliefs, Attitudes, and Knowledge* (San Francisco: Jossey-Bass, 1977).

15. The three descriptions that follow are direct quotes.

16. https://www.geteducated.com/careers/highest-paying-associate-degree-jobs.

17. C. Hall Dillon, "Military Training for Civilian Careers," *Occupational Outlook Quarterly*, Spring 2007.

18. "Project Build Minnesota," Builders Association of the Twin Cities.

19. Kevin Fleming, "Success in the Economy," YouTube.

20. Kersten and Pearlstein.

21. Nicholas Eberstadt, *Men Without Work: America's Invisible Crisis* (West Conshohocken, PA: Templeton, 2016).

22. P. McDonough, "TV Viewing Among Kids at an Eight-Year High," Nielsen, 2009.

23. North Minneapolis has the largest black population in the city.

24. Kate Hardiman, "Proposed Trump Budget Expands Access to Vocational Programs," *Washington Examiner*, February 16, 2018.

25. Katherine Kersten, "Postsecondary Education for Non-Dummies," (Minneapolis) *Star Tribune*, July 16, 2017.

Chapter 4

The Growing Power of Debt

Carlita is a single woman in her 20s, one of four adult siblings plus a husband with whom I met in a church basement to talk about several of the issues addressed in these pages. She has a four-year degree from a private institution, as was the case with everyone else around the table. We had just started talking about college debt when she said: "If I could make the decision over again, I would, in a heartbeat. I would start at a community college, because the debt I incurred, and still have, really has been prohibitive for me. I would have liked to continue my education in graduate school, but I don't want to pay off loans until I'm 60."

At which point Carlita's sister Kaylee jumped in and talked about how she also has a baccalaureate from a private university, as does her husband, and that they lived in her parents' home for two years after getting married because of college debt.

"I've had a full-time job since college, a good one, but I've also had second and third jobs. People look at me and ask why I work on weekends—why do I have another job? I tell them I don't have an option, as I don't want to still have this debt when I'm of retirement age." Kaylee and Josh recently bought a house of their own, which she unsurprisingly acknowledged was "going to be a difficult road."

I didn't want to pry (too much), so I asked, "If you want to give me numbers, fine. But I'm not asking."

"Well, mine was over $100,000, and my husband Josh has his loan, as well."

To which I exclaimed for one of the few times in my life, "Oh, my heart."

Josh's loan was $40,000, even though he started by getting a two-year degree from a community college. Trouble was, he did his final two years at a for-profit university, which, for good measure, was subsequently closed down. "Looking back," he said, "I wish I would have gone to a state school for my last two years as I would have less debt."

At some point Carlita said she was, in fact, planning to "put away a little money." But that, in "big part" because of college debt, "I definitely don't feel in a place to buy a home, have a family, or take care of somebody."

As for brother Ryan, at 30 the oldest sibling and with debt of his own: "You just can't do all the things you want to do as you get older. I hope that young people graduating from high school meet with financial aid counselors and try to project what their payments will be when they're finished with school. The unfortunate thing is that you're not always thinking long term when you're that age, right? They just think their job will pay for it." Or as sister Kerry put it, "You sign all these things when you're 18, 19 years old saying you're going to pay back all that money, but then you come to realize how much it actually is."

Catrin Thorman (somehow not related to Kaylee, Kerry, and Carlita) described herself in another interview as fitting the "stereotype of someone with a four-year degree who was in debt when I graduated" and who "went into panic mode" that summer. "Oh, my goodness. What am I going to do? Where am I going to work with a political science degree so that I can pay back the school I attended out of state? It was a private college that got me for every dollar I had and will continue doing so in the coming years."

There's good news, though. For the first time, at 27 years old, Thorman is working in a field in which her political science degree aligns with what she is doing professionally. Even better news is that she had just become engaged to a man who has an A.A.S. degree plus several certificates in information technology and (pause) no debt. "But I feel the burden of being the only one in the marriage with all that debt, knowing we will have to handle it together. That's another important thing for people to consider about two-year degrees versus four-year degrees: Money is already a tense subject with couples, so my future husband being debt free brings a sigh of relief, even though we will have to worry about my debt."

And then there is the business owner who talked about how "debt is a big deal; it's a lot of stress." He was referring not just to the difficulty or inability of a husband and wife buying a house but to "what it does to a person's life, whether they meet somebody, or even whether they're able to conceive. I mean there's a whole bunch of things going on."

The man who said this, Mitch Davis, owns a dairy operation in southern Minnesota with 20,000 animals. He added another dimension to matters of debt by noting how the academic and training demands on veterinarians are the equal of those of medical doctors, with educational expenses for both groups similar. "But when veterinarians get out of school, they get $65,000 and they probably have $250,000 to $300,000 in debt. And you wonder why we're short of large animal vets, which is a big thing in terms of world imports and exports of food."

Having a hard time grasping such a huge cleavage between income and student debt, I did some checking, and Davis was fundamentally right. According to one website, it's not uncommon for veterinarians to leave school up to $250,000 in debt, and that includes just loans taken during their four years of vet school; it does not include any debt from their undergraduate years or whatever postdoctoral work they may have had.[1] According to another website, veterinarians in the United States earn about $72,000 a year.[2] In a few moments, we will discuss degrees of fear, or their relative lack, in different student loan situations. Let's just say the repayment challenge facing veterinarians is as frightening as for any group I know.

Wait: Here's student debt to sink your teeth into even deeper. The *Wall Street Journal* has just reported that a 37-year-old orthodontist in Utah, Dr. Mike Meru, owed $1,060,945 in student loans as of May 24, 2018. The paper provided the exact date for what he owed as interest was increasing his obligation by $130 a day. Yet Dr. Meru, who attended the University of Southern California for seven years, is not alone. "Due to escalating and easy credit," the *Journal* said, "the U.S. has 101 people who owe at least $1 million in federal student loans, according to the Education Department."[3] I would have said impossible to imagine, but I would have been wrong.

Time to take a breath. College debt is not necessarily an out-of-bounds burden for most people, much less a "crushing headache," as one interviewee described student debt levels. Average college debt across the nation hovers around $30,000, which surely is not sofa change and may intimidate. But I start from the premise that something is wrong if a person doesn't value his or her education as much as the price of a modest Ford, which the last time I checked was between $20,000 and $30,000 for a Fusion.

As for the possibility of intimidation, and in fairness, I appreciate how it can be inversely related to a family's income and wealth. Though it's also true that very bright, low-income students frequently win financial aid packages, even at the most expensive private schools, that entail little eventual debt.

But what about interest? When it's written or said that a person has taken out, say, $30,000 in loans, is it commonly assumed that $30,000 is the total to be paid back, with interest already factored in? Or is interest not yet accounted for, meaning the borrower is on the hook for measurably more than $30,000? I may be wrong, but after reading a lot of popular and other accounts about student loans, my sense is most references to student debt ignore the reality of interest, thus underplaying how difficult making good on loans may be.

As I write, here are what various interest rates and resulting monthly payments look like when $30,000 is the principal.[4]

- A $30,000 loan at 5.0 percent, repaid over 10 years, would result in monthly payments of $318, totaling $38,183. Or $8,183 in interest.
- A $30,000 loan at 6.8 percent, repaid over 10 years, would result in monthly payments of $345, totaling $41,429. Or $11,429 in interest.
- And a $30,000 loan at 7.9 percent, repaid over 10 years, would result in monthly payments of $362, totaling $43,888. Or $13,488 in interest.

These rates are not imagined of whole cloth, but rather are fixed rates for Federal Perkins Loans (5.0 percent); Federal Stafford Loans (6.8 percent); and Federal PLUS Loans (7.9 percent). It's also worth noting that graduates may claim an annual tax deduction of up to $2,500 for interest paid on student loan debt.

An aside that suggests why I may instinctively focus on the same $30,000 just cited several times.

Between my undergraduate and graduate school loans, I seem to recall borrowing between $15,000 and $20,000. Conservatively, let's say the total was $15,000, broken down $5,000 for my B.A., which I received in 1970, and $10,000 for my Ph.D., which I received in 1980. What do those numbers inflate to now?

According to the Bureau of Labor Statistics,[5] $5,000 in January 1970 had the buying power of $32,787 in January 2018. Spooky.

And $10,000 in January 1980 was the equivalent of $31,860 in January 2018. Spooky redux.

I'm obliged to add here that I needed my parents' help at one point in paying off the tiny monthly payments of the first loan, mainly because my first real job, as a reporter in Binghamton, New York, paid $1.85 an hour, which was the minimum wage in the state at the time. This is another way of acknowledging that I appreciate how financially tough it can be for many former college students and their parents currently, which is not necessarily to say unreasonably or unfairly tough.

But a key complication: What about postgraduate studies these days? While approximately $30,000 in undergraduate loans does not worry me if a person has no plans of pursuing a graduate or professional degree, it does if they do. Tori Roloff, an exceptionally talented young woman who served as my intern for a summer and who was entering her sophomore year at the University of Virginia, framed matters well. I had just asked what she saw herself doing about three years hence.

"I think I eventually want to go to law school," Roloff said, "but I don't want to do that right away, because I don't want to go from one debt to another right away. It's a huge investment to make, so I want to first see if I'm happy with what I might be doing without a law degree. If I am, I wouldn't need to go and get one." Suffice it to say, she would make a quality contribution to justice if she did go.

One more caveat, an important and particularly subtle one before moving on: It would be a mistake to assume that students graduating with the biggest debts usually wind up with the toughest financial plights. They generally don't, because they tend to graduate from the most-respected institutions, win the best-paying jobs, and contend with unemployment less often. This is the case for men and women earning both undergraduate and graduate degrees.

Counterintuitively, students who wind up in the most trying financial holes are disproportionately those who enrolled in community colleges—the very places I've been applauding. This is also the case with people, generally no longer teenagers, who enroll in for-profit schools. To what extent might this community college fact of economic life undermine my argument? Little, if any, as note I use the words "enrolled in," not "graduated from," above. The difference can be immense.

I also didn't say anything just now about what kinds of community college programs students chose. Did they take only or mostly general courses which left them largely bereft of marketable skills, perhaps along with résumés announcing they might do poorly following through if they left school before graduating? Or did they take the kinds of technical and career-focused courses I've been talking about, finishing with the kind of two-year degree or shorter certificate that employers value? The answer is manifest: There's an ocean of difference between pursuing the kinds of community college programs that lead to solid middle-class careers and then graduating, and doing neither.

Susan Dynarski is a professor of education, public policy, and economics at the University of Michigan.[6] She wrote in 2015 that loan defaults are "concentrated among the millions of students who drop out without a degree, and they tend to have smaller debts." Or similarly, "Students who attended a two- or four-year college without earning a degree are struggling to find well-paying work to pay off the debt they accumulated."

Or, as my adviser once advised, "The idea is to finish." And as an interviewee contended, when students drop out, particularly from four-year programs, it's as if employers and others see "big scarlet letters on their chests." Under such circumstances, it's easy to see how young people can think poorly of themselves and fall into funks and depression.

As for students who do earn bachelor's degrees, Dynarski added, the "vast majority" are doing very nicely. "Only two percent of undergraduates borrow more than $50,000, and they also aren't the ones who tend to have problems with their debt." Might this latter conclusion by Dynarski undermine my argument that debt is, in fact, causing many students and parents to rethink post–high school plans?

No, again, as just because the "vast majority" of loan holders with baccalaureates are "doing very well," as she puts it, that doesn't mean that acquiring tens of thousands of dollars in debt is an attractive prospect for most people. Her conclusion, moreover, at least as captured in a couple of sentences, does not speak to the fear many high school students have about picking up a ton of debt, even if they are otherwise confident they will eventually succeed greatly. Now imagine parents' possible fright if they have more than one child in college at the same time, or on the cusp.[7] I trust Dynarski understands that fear is frequently robust.

In keeping with "on the one hand" and the "other" reactions, a 2018 survey[8] found that a quarter of respondents admitted "they would have attended a less expensive school if they knew what they know now about the debt they'd incur." How should this be interpreted? That a quarter of respondents is a frighteningly high proportion? Or that it's an encouraging small one? I would say it's more the latter.

But then, again, the article reported that "46 percent of college graduates who ended up taking out a student loan suffer from student loan regret." Certainly, a more sobering proportion.

How do student loan forgiveness programs fit in all of this? Sometimes snugly, often not. Or, as teased on the Internet:

"If You Have Any Student Loans, You May Qualify For Partial Or COMPLETE Loan Forgiveness $0 Payments! Find out in minutes if you are eligible for one of the many government backed programs. 2 Min Call Can Save You Thousands. Call Now to Check Eligibility!"[9]

There are partial and total federal forgiveness programs tied to specific fields pursued, such as teaching, health, or public service. There are programs based on a percentage of people's discretionary income. Or if they are in the military. Or if they're disabled. There are federal programs that kick in after certain numbers of years. There also are state-based loan-forgiveness programs such as for young dentists in Ohio and young farmers in New York.

Yes, without question, it pays to check one's eligibility, as the Internet ad above pitches. But if I were back in school, I would like to think I would take the safest route and assume that whatever loans I took out, plus whatever interest payments accrued, would remain my obligation entirely, and I would map out my life accordingly. I would like to think that.

A final ounce of forgiveness. The *Wall Street Journal* story about Dr. Meru concluded by noting how the balance of what he owes "will keep growing through the 25-year life of the repayment plan until it reaches $2 million." That amount will then be forgiven; arguably a pretty good deal after a quarter century of big monthly bills. But as the story added, at current tax rates, such governmental grace "could cost Mr. Meru more than $700,000 in income tax payments."[10] Coming and going.

All this is a good lead-in to my three discussions with Ben Wright, the former president of a demanding two-year technology school in Minneapolis formerly known as Dunwoody Institute, which in 2002 started offering a demanding four-year technology degree as well, with the institution now known as Dunwoody College. One of our exchanges involved just the two of us, with the other two parts of roundtables. More than once he elaborated on how "for the first time in maybe 15 years, people outside the world of vocational technical education were paying some attention to the economic opportunities" made possible by such programs—the "incredible job opportunities that exist for people with technical skills." The fact that Wright holds a doctorate in history from the University of Wisconsin, not any technical degree from anyplace, deepens what he had to say.

"For many years, we have been encouraging everyone to go to college, which always meant a four-year as opposed to a two-year college, with the expectation that all sorts of opportunities would open to them. And I've seen more and more young people following that path, often taking more than four years to complete their degree but then not employed in jobs commensurate with their education and its expense. So, after feeling as though I had been crying in the wilderness, it has begun to feel as if other people are paying attention, too."

I reminded Dunwoody's former president that he had been quick to say several months earlier that a significant reason for society's shifting view was that so many kids were going into debt and so many parents were eating up their retirement savings. "One of the truisms of selling higher education," he went on, "has been that people with four-year degrees do better economically. But increasingly I'm wondering if that data is really old, because we have to include the mounting size of individual and family debt in assessing economic payoffs of four-year degrees, and I'm not convinced that researchers have been doing that." There's certainly no incentive, he added, "for people employed in higher education to look at data which might discourage young people from pursuing traditional four-year degrees."

"Especially if faculty are not tenured," I added, with equal parts glibness and seriousness.

A few moments later, historian Wright emphasized that he "definitely was not anti–liberal arts and definitely not anti-four-year institutions." If young people choose to pursue such an academic path, "I just think they need to do so with their eyes open, knowing what they want to get out of it. This idea that education should be separated from vocation is a phony one, even where the liberal arts are concerned. It's not one or the other. It's important to think very intentionally about both getting a good education and preparing yourself for financial independence after you're done. That means keeping an eye on that debt. 'What's going to help me pay it off?'"

Of more than small semantic interest, I noted above that Dunwoody is no longer an "Institute" but a "College." Why? One reason, according to Wright, is that for 30 years Dunwoody "offered a youth career awareness program aimed at inner-city kids, introducing them to technical occupations and careers. They were graduating from high school, but they weren't coming to Dunwoody. We found out when we interviewed parents they didn't think it was a 'college.' The Massachusetts *Institute* of Technology is certainly a college. The California *Institute* of Technology is certainly a college. But if many parents and others weren't thinking of Dunwoody as a *college*, they weren't going to give it a moment's thought, as their aspirations were higher. This is the case especially if you've never had any family members go to college."

Returning to return-on-investment studies: As it happens, two very good recent ones have taken student debt explicitly into account. Does this represent a change of course compared to what Wright contended has historically been the case? I would suspect yes.

One study was conducted in 2017 by Amanda L. Griffith, an economist at Wake Forest University, "No Four-Year Degree Required: A Look at a Selection of In-Demand Careers in Minnesota."[11] This superb paper showed how Minnesotans who choose two-year degrees, one-year certificates, and apprenticeships often do better than counterparts with four-year degrees when it comes to lifetime earnings. A major reason is the lower costs of entering non-four-year technical jobs and careers, especially when much smaller student debt routinely associated with them is accounted for.

Among fields Griffith examined were registered nursing, construction, carpentry, plumbing, heating and air-conditioning (HVAC), computer numerical control programming (CNC), electrical power-line installing, and working as a millwright. "Positions like these," she wrote, "are not only currently in demand but are projected to continue to increase over the next decade. In addition, many of these fields have an aging population of workers, meaning that many jobs will be opening up in the next decade for replacement by new and younger workers." Vitally, Griffith also wrote that estimated median lifetime earnings for people in jobs she highlighted could exceed the median lifetime earnings of counterparts holding four-year degrees "by as much as 61 percent."

A second, national study, published in 2016, is "Are College Costs Worth It? How Ability, Major, and Debt Affect the Returns to Schooling," by Douglas A. Webber, a Temple University economist.[12] It, too, is first-rate and essential for better grasping and evaluating the claims and counterclaims made in this and other chapters.

Using the life-cycle earnings simulation model he developed, Webber opens by acknowledging that college debt has been rising steadily with students now "burdened by an average of $30,000" in obligations. (That number again.) Begged, he says, is the question: "Is taking on substantial student loan debt to (possibly) obtain a college degree a sound financial proposition? Unsurprisingly, this simple question has a complicated answer which depends on a variety of factors, such as the student's major, ability level, and probability of completing a degree, among many others." (I don't think it's a simple question at all.)

Keep in mind here, Webber reports that 40 percent of baccalaureate seekers—a very large share of whom hold loans—will not graduate within six years of starting college. He correctly calls this a "critical but often overlooked factor when evaluating the financial value of attending college." Even so, he critically concludes that graduating from college is a "good financial proposition under most scenarios, even when taking into account the uncertainty of actually completing a degree."

Webber goes on: "For an individual with average ability, the value added of the vast majority of majors is worth well beyond the typical costs associated with a four-year public institution." Begged this time are questions about students who wind up paying much more than "the typical costs associated with a four-year public institution." Students, for example, who attend colleges and universities with hard-to-believe tuition rates and fees. Webber adds that even for students with lower levels of ability (in the lowest quartile), most four-year degrees are "worth the usual investment." But if they pay "substantially more than" average costs, "they may not see their investment pay off until much later in life, and, depending on their major, the degree may never pay itself off." Overall, Webber estimates the "present discounted value of attending college for the median student to vary between $85,000 and $300,000 depending on the student's major."

Statistically building on the spirit of Wright, Griffith, and Webber's arguments are fascinating data regarding growth and decline in various undergraduate majors over different time spans this century. It would be a reach to say they have been primarily the result of debt-related fears, as the nation's economic health at various points certainly was a more potent driver. But then, again, and quite obviously, people have crisper concerns about paying back loans of any kind if they are concerned about finding or keeping a job. And hence they are more interested in what they view as more remunerative majors than they might be otherwise.

According to the National Center for Education Statistics, while the number of bachelor's degrees awarded increased by 32 percent between 2004–2005 and 2014–2015, "there was substantial variation among the different fields of study as well as shifts in the patterns of change during this time period."[13]

Keeping in mind the Great Recession hit in 2008:

- The number of bachelor's degrees awarded in computer and information sciences decreased 27 percent between 2004–2005 and 2009–2010, but then increased 50 percent between 2009–2010 and 2014–2015.
- The number of bachelor's degrees in the combined fields of engineering and engineering technologies increased 12 percent between 2004–2005 and 2009–2010 but then increased a further 30 percent between 2009–2010 and 2014–2015.
- The number of bachelor's degrees conferred in the health professions and related programs increased by 61 percent (pretty sizable) between 2004–2005 and 2009–2010, and then by 67 percent (even more sizably) between 2009–2010 and 2014–2015.
- In contrast, the number of bachelor's degrees in English language and literature/letters was 14 percent lower in 2014–2015 than in 2009–2010, and the number of degrees in philosophy and religious studies was 11 percent lower over that period. Perhaps the only surprise in these two categories is that the dips were as small as they were.

In our conversation in Washington, education scholar and writer Chester E. Finn Jr. said, "Fear of debt is driving a number of people into majors they see as leading to good salaries." Maybe not a complete explanation, but a weighty one.

This might be an apt spot to note that "over 71 percent of STEM workers with some college but no degree make more than the average for workers with some college but no degree." And that 66 percent of STEM workers "with an associate degree make more money than the average for workers with an associate's degree."[14]

It's also an apt time to acknowledge I haven't said anything about why tuition rates have gone up as much as they have—faster than inflation. Probing that question is a job for another day, but it's no leap to say it's combinations of state cutbacks in support of higher education and/or large sums of federal loan dollars inviting colleges and universities to be less frugal than they otherwise might. And/or talented faculty being paid what they deserve. And/or many of those same faculty teaching too few classes. And/or failure to take more than meager advantage of technological advances in instruction. And/or too many governmental rules and regulations. And/or too many well-paid administrators, partially because of all those rules and regs. And/or excessive student fondness for fancy facilities, and so on.

Sandra Kresbach is the executive director of the American Technical Education Association. We've met her several times already, most pertinently last chapter when she spoke about the wisdom of seeking a one-year certificate as a safety net if a person has debt and other bills to pay and a life to lead but painfully finds that a four-year degree, or an unsuccessful quest for one, is insufficiently helpful. Here's more of what she said during our conversation. We had been talking about student (and parental) debt, and I had just asked her for examples of the kinds of fields in which a certificate could be the ticket.

"I would do HR, human resources," she said. "I'd look at the financial world for a lower-level accounting certificate. I was just at a cybersecurity summit, and certificates work in that world. There's a huge employer base for it, and it's intriguing. I would flip to the technical. I would flip through websites of two-year colleges and look at career worlds you would like to function in. What are those first jobs? What are those first certificates?"

Kresbach also talked about employers being interested in people with technical aptitudes, even if they don't have technical certification. She speculated how students and others could take advantage of this. On another occasion, she talked about how holding a job thanks to a certificate "reduces stress" in a person's life.

I've already noted a couple of times the kinds of jobs for which a one-year (or two-year) certificate might apply—fields such as cosmetology, massage therapy, and various computer-related specialties, especially cybersecurity, which does seem to be a higher-profile and more important line of work by the day and threat. Let me add a few more, most of which tie more directly to what Sandra has in mind in her comments above. The suffix in each example is "Proficiency Certificate," as in "Baseball Proficiency Certificate," which I deleted to avoid irritating redundancy. The fields are drawn from a listing posted by the Community College of Philadelphia, which I found by scrolling through a listing of websites:

"Accounting Paraprofessional; Automotive Service (I) and Automotive Service (II); Medical Insurance Billing; Paralegal Studies; Patient Service Representative; and Web Development. Along with other computer-related jobs, including Cybersecurity (I) and Cybersecurity (II)."

Reinforcing much of what has come before, and not just in this chapter, an interviewee in the construction industry told me about how a colleague has three sons. "Two went on to get bachelor's degrees in the liberal arts. The third went into a technical field and makes more than the other two and has zero debt. My friend likes telling this story all the time. It's a classic example of what you're talking about."

Let's conclude the chapter with comments by three other interviewees. Fred Senn is an advertising executive; John Slama is Argosy University campus president in Eagan, Minnesota; and Larry Pogemiller is Minnesota's commissioner of higher education. Argosy is a national for-profit university with programs ranging from two-year to doctoral.

"Instead of getting out there and tearing the world apart at 22," Fred Senn said, "kids now often have $30,000 of debt to pay off before they can think about doing things like buying a house. That's too much debt for a 22-year-old."

I said $30,000 was about average for men and women completing four-year degrees, or at least after four years questing for one. Fred suggested that I pull together a publication (principally digital, I presume) that listed all the jobs in the country available to people with two-year degrees and what those jobs paid. "We've got to wake up kids, we've got to get 17-year-olds thinking."

This complemented something John Slama had said a few months earlier during a roundtable discussion:

"A colleague and I recently sat in a high school classroom," John said, "with a group of seniors getting prepared for graduation as part of a Rotary Club initiative. We were talking to them about career options and what they wanted to do. What were their plans? And encouraging them to have plans. One of the things we noticed is that all these kids had laptops. So, I asked if anyone had ever heard of deed.com or indeed.com, two job websites in Minnesota. No. They asked what were they?"

Within minutes, John reported, "they were all looking at career information they had no idea was there. It's wonderful information. And before you knew it, they were fully engaged with how much salary people make in different jobs. What kinds of education do they require, two-year degrees included, and what kinds of careers could they get into? I mean, information is there, but so few kids had any kind of plan."

Larry Pogemiller and I were talking about student debt when he mentioned a student he met at Bemidji State University in northern Minnesota. "He told me he was a junior and was $40,000 in debt, and I wanted to go, 'Oh, my God,' as he was likely to wind up about $53,000 in debt. A person doesn't have to go so much in debt to get a degree from Bemidji"—a fine place though it might be, as the commissioner and I would agree. "We need to educate better how to think about money and how to use money."

Elsewhere in our conversation, Larry, who is an old friend, talked more specifically about what he saw as government's role in helping college students avoid winding up in overly deep holes. "Trying to inform people and protect them from taking on too much debt is a role of government—not that government should be anti-debt when it comes to college debt, because there's a lot of evidence it works out well for a lot of people." How much debt is a right amount? "The way we talk about it in the biz, is don't take on more debt than you're going to make in your first job, with the exception if a person wants to be a doctor or some other professional, as $200,000 in loans is often what it takes."

Putting aside the difficulty in predicting several years in advance how much money a person might make in his or her first job, somehow this rule of thumb worked out for me. I estimate my previously mentioned $5,000 undergraduate loan roughly matched my first real job as a reporter, for an independently owned morning newspaper, at $1.85 an hour in 1971, with a raise to $2.50 within the year when the paper was purchased by Gannett. I can't believe I lived on weekly paychecks of something like $74 to start and that I had enough disposable income to have a drink or two with my colleagues a couple days a week after finishing police checks at 1 a.m. (A more precise $74.11 just popped into my head.)

Larry Pogemiller went on: "Where do we say this is a matter of personal responsibility? It's really hard for government to decide at what point it has some responsibility to protect people from themselves. There's never a perfect answer to that, but we have to keep working at it. You can set something up where the average works, but then you get a person who does something, and you go, 'Oh my God, how did we let that happen?'"

NOTES

1. Doctor.org/cost-vs-reward-of-veterinary-school.
2. Payscale.com.
3. Josh Mitchell, "The $1 Million Student Loan: 'Should I Be Doing This?'" *Wall Street Journal*, May 26–27, 2018. Regarding interest rates, Mitchell writes: "In the 2004–2005 school year, the rate for college and graduate students was 2.77%. The following school year, Mr. Meru's first at USC, rates jumped to 4.75% for his loans. Those turned out to be the cheapest of the 50 loans he needed to finance his education." Add to this the fact that, according to Mitchell, "Dental school is the costliest higher-education program in the U.S. . . . The USC program now costs $91,000 a year, and $137,000 when living expenses are included."
4. Fin Aid: The SmartStudent Guide to Financial Aid. http://www.finaid.org/calculators/scripts/loanpayments.egi.
5. Bls.gov/data/inflation_calculator.htm.
6. Susan Dynarski, "Why Students with Smallest Debts Have the Larger Problem," *New York Times*, August 31, 2015. Also helpful is Dynarski's article, "New Data Gives Clearer Picture of Student Debt," *New York Times*, September 10, 2015. As is Adam Looney and Constantine Yannelis, "A crisis in student loans? How changes in the characteristics of borrowers and in the institutions they attended contributed to rising loan defaults," Brookings, Fall 2015.
7. After writing this, I was informed by my colleague, Prof. Kent Kaiser, that the "way federal aid works, there is an expected parental contribution. It is divided by the number of kids in college. Therefore, it makes sense to have kids one right after another—twins or triplets, if possible—to make the family contribution the smallest possible and to obtain the greatest financial aid. People think they're being fiscally smart by spacing out their children, but that's the worst thing to do." While this qualification, I trust, is all true, it doesn't mean that parents wouldn't still be hit with intimidatingly big college bills. While not as huge, they might be hardly less scary.

8. Zoya Gervis, "Young Americans Suffering from Serious Case of Student Loan Regret," originally published by South West News Service, June 25, 2018. The survey was conducted by "OnePoll in conjunction with EDvestinU, the national nonprofit student loan program of the New Hampshire Higher Education Loans Corporation (NHHELCO)," and involved "2,000 graduates."

9. Federal Student Loan Helpers, Delray Beach, FL.

10. Mitchell.

11. Amanda L. Griffith, "No Four-Year Degree Required: A Look at a Selection of In-Demand Jobs in Minnesota," Center of the American Experiment, Golden Valley, MN, September 2017.

12. Douglas A. Webber, "Are College Costs Worth It? How Ability, Major, and Debt Affect the Returns to Schooling, *Economics of Education Review* 53 (2016), 296–310.

13. U.S. Department of Education, National Center for Education Statistics (2018), *Digest of Education Statistics, 2016* (NCES 2017-094).

14. Anthony P. Carnevale, Nicole Smith, and Michelle Melton, *STEM*, Georgetown University Center on Education and the Workforce, October 20, 2011.

Chapter 5

Potential Economic Detours

American economic growth and prosperity are already constrained by too few skilled men and women in the trades, especially in construction and manufacturing. This problem threatens to grow worse as highly skilled baby boomers continue to retire at enormous rates but are not succeeded by adequate numbers of sufficiently trained younger people.

Or, if you will, "We exist in an economy that competes on talent. Yet we have jobs without people and people without jobs. Business growth is hindered because we do not have the right talent needed to take on new businesses at the right time."[1]

Let's begin following up on these points with extended excerpts from a conversation I had with Darlene Miller, owner of Permac Industries, a precision manufacturing business in Burnsville, Minnesota, and someone I've mentioned several times now. While serving on the President's Council for Jobs and Competitiveness during the Obama administration, she conceived Right Skills Now, a program—in 13 states at last count—that addresses the shortage of computer numerical control (CNC) machine operators via "16 to 24 weeks of hands-on CNC operator immersion learning experience[s] provided by community colleges."[2] Yes, she's impressive.

After pleasantries, I asked what her company did, exactly.

"Permac is a precision machining company that does very complex, very high technology work mainly for aerospace, defense, and food and beverage industries. We certainly can do other things such as medical devices, but it's always either a single component, or a small set of assembly parts that go into something larger, whether it's an airplane, or missile, or a submarine." Or a Coke machine, I noted.

"The materials we use are not easy things to machine, so we really need the best of equipment, the best of tooling, and the best of talent to make these new products. We do a lot of new products which are tougher to do but can be quite profitable. We have about 30 people and run three shifts. If we could hire eight or ten more people today we'd do it. We have our hands out all the time."

Pursuing the obvious, I asked if Permac was prevented from growing bigger because of a lack of skilled people for these jobs.

"Absolutely," was Miller's one-word answer, followed by "It's really difficult to find machinists who have experience in programming and setup." A main reason, she said, was the failure of schools, including many technical schools, to spend enough time and effort teaching math, especially trigonometry. She also spoke of how "our technology changes every year, but much of the equipment used by schools is very outdated, and teachers often are people who last worked in machining 20 years ago."

A few minutes later, after talking about the satisfaction of making the triggers that enable oxygen masks in airplanes to drop down or medical devices that save lives, I asked why it was so difficult to get stories like these to young people so they might get animated and say, "Hey, there may be something for me in this line of work." (More on occupational and artisanal fulfillment in chapter 7.) As with other people throughout the book, she cited the business community for not getting the word out, especially in terms of working with schools.

"We haven't worked with high schools or middle schools, which is where you really need to start. We need to bring parents to our plants and show them what we're doing and how clean, how spotless, and how much brainpower we need, because they don't have a clue about what's going on behind those doors." Yet while the *insides* of plants may be spiffy, a senior official of the National Association of Manufacturers, in a meeting a few months later, conceded plants' and factories' often drab and windowless *outsides* can look anything but welcoming. What to do beyond more inviting landscaping?

Darlene Miller continued: "Probably 80 percent of kids who go to college also have no clue, this time about what they want to be when they grow up. That makes it easy for school counselors who can say, 'Just go to a four-year college. You'll find your path. It'll all work out in the end. Life will be beautiful.' With manufacturing or any of the trades it's specific. You're going to be a machinist. You're going to be a plumber. You're going to be a carpenter. But counselors don't know enough about these avenues to even help direct them."

In time, I got to another heart of the matter: How is the shortage of sophisticated machinists and other well-trained men and women in trades hurting the economy?

"Regardless of the industry, we won't continue to grow. We won't be able to build enough cars, enough airplanes. But it's not just manufacturing, it's also not having anyone fix plumbing in our homes. It's going to take six months to get someone to do a new roof."

Hyperbole for effect? Yes. But then there was another business owner, Myron Moser, whom we also met earlier, who spoke of a friend, the CFO of a large automotive group, who said she had openings for 77 mechanics, and that if she had them today, she'd hire them today. Moser also talked about the immense amount of money a big bakery—the kind that makes buns for McDonald's—would lose every hour if one of its major pieces of equipment went down and there were too few specifically trained people in the vicinity to fix it quickly. Moser said the loss would be about $100,000 an hour—a number I can't confirm but which certainly is impressive.

One more exchange with Darlene Miller. She had just talked about how much manufacturing had changed over the previous 25 years: "When I got into the business, we were making simple components. Many employees got out of their pickup trucks, came in, and functioned. Now it's totally the opposite." To which I wondered how many young people simply would be scared away by the intricacy of it all. To which Miller said, "You're right, it could be intimidating, but kids tend to find it fascinating because they're looking at screens all day as it is. These kids are talented when it comes to computers, so much more than people our age."

We'll get back to what other interviewees said about the importance of expertly trained men and women in manufacturing and other fields and trades, especially with 10,000 baby boomers, give or take, hitting 65 and potentially retiring every 24 hours. "As the year 2011 began on January 1," the Pew Research Center reported, "the oldest members of the baby boom Generation celebrated their sixty-fifth birthday. In fact, on that day, today, and for every day of the next 19 years, 10,000 baby boomers will reach 65."[3]

There has been no shortage of major studies on this and related topics in recent years, along with a great deal of substantial journalistic analysis. That's where we'll go next, starting with a report released by the Manufacturing Institute and Deloitte in 2015, *The Skills Gaps in U.S. Manufacturing 2015 and Beyond*.[4] We'll intersperse reports and analyses with comments by other interviewees as we go along.

Right at the start, the Manufacturing Institute and Deloitte study projects how 3.5 million manufacturing jobs "likely" would need to be filled over the decade beginning in 2015, but because of the "skills gap," 2 million of them would go unfilled.[5] Two major dynamics would contribute to the shortage: the retirement of 2.7 million men and women, large numbers of whom would be previously mentioned baby boomers, born between 1946 and 1964; with "natural business expansion" leading to another 700,000 unfilled positions.[6] The report immediately cited four additional factors for the gap: "loss of embedded knowledge" because of all the movement of experienced workers; negative impressions about manufacturing on the part of young people; a lack of STEM skills; and the decline of technical education offerings in high schools.

How much might the skills gap diminish what U.S. businesses could do? In a survey tied to the report, 82 percent of responding executives said they believed it would "impact their ability to meet customer demand." And 78 percent said it would "impact their ability to implement new technologies and increase productivity." From another angle, the Manufacturing Institute and Deloitte report cited a study that estimated "average" manufacturers in the United States losing 11 percent of their annual earnings because of talent shortages,[7] with another study estimating an average loss of $14,000 per each unfilled position.[8] All substantial hits.

In another report, this one released in 2005, the National Academy of Sciences, the National Academy of Engineering, and the Institute of Medicine "undertook a study of America's evolving competitiveness in the global economy." The resulting publication, *Rising Above the Gathering Storm*,[9] opened by noting how the United States "takes deserved pride in the vitality of its economy, which forms the foundation of our high quality of life, our national security, and our hope that our children and grandchildren will inherit ever-greater opportunities." Nonetheless, about 500 pages later, it concluded: "Without a renewed effort to bolster the foundations of our competitiveness, we can expect to lose our privileged position."

Five years later, in 2010, many of the truly distinguished men and women who participated in the 2005 project reassembled and produced a follow-up, *Rising Above the Gathering Storm Revisited*,[10] which concluded that not nearly enough progress had been made in a range of scientific, educational, governmental, and other areas. Disconcerting as the update was, it was not surprising for no other reason than not many national reports conclude by declaring victory.

Problems identified in 2005 were insufficiently solved by 2010 because they were intrinsically tough, possibly compounded by national embarrassment, as when it was noted that "The World Economic Forum ranks the United States forty-eighth in quality of mathematics and science education."[11] Or even more pertinently to what we've been dissecting, "The United States has fallen from first to eleventh place in the OECD in the fraction [of] 25- to 34-year-olds that has graduated high school," while the "older portion of the U.S. workforce ranks first among OECD populations of the same age."[12] (OECD is the acronym for the Organization for Economic Co-Operation and Development.) For our purposes, though, one paragraph stands out in the Academies' 2010 report.

"It should be reiterated that the need to strengthen science and math education in the nation's public schools is not simply to produce more graduates possessing the qualifications needed to pursue degrees and careers in science and engineering. The spectrum of jobs that is available to high school as well as college graduates is increasingly demanding at least rudimentary skills in these fields." I would like to think that if this were written now instead of 2010, the last sentence would refer not just to high school and (presumably) four-year graduates, but specifically also to recipients of associate of arts degrees and one-year and two-year certificates, as well as to graduates of apprenticeship programs and veterans who learned occupational skills in the military.

Let's get back to what several interviewees had to say about key economic issues before returning to scholars and researchers.

As with Darlene Miller, Myron Moser owns a technologically sophisticated business, Hartfiel Automation, "a specialized high-tech provider of pneumatics, motion, mobile control and robotic solutions" with headquarters in Eden Prairie, Minnesota. We've met him several times already, most recently when he talked about the stratospheric costs of never-made hamburger buns.

In our conversation, I had just pointed out what some people, such as me on occasion, might view as a contradiction: "People in your position say we don't have enough well-trained employees. But others say advanced technology gets rid of jobs, hence we don't need more people. What is it, sir?"

"That's an oversimplification," Moser said, and went on: "It's like the argument about how automobiles put buggy whip manufacturers out of business. We just retrained those workers, and they started building autos instead of buggy whips."

I countered by saying I assumed it wasn't difficult in a cognitive sense for most people to move from making buggy whips to working on an assembly line making Model Ts. It likely wasn't as enjoyable or satisfying working on an assembly line instead of as an artisan, but the switch wasn't unduly demanding intellectually. Yet it *can* be cognitively challenging to do many current jobs resulting from automation. One reason for saying this is that I don't have many if any technical skills myself, and the same is true for a lot of people, as they're just not built that way. What's to be done?

But a lot of people *are* built that way, Moser countered, which is, in fact, the case. Recall what Darlene Miller said a few moments ago about young people having a much better grasp of how computers work than older people. Her full quotation, which is not included above, ended with the cryptic line, "It's their brain power in the computer." I don't know if that's exactly how she intended to phrase what she had in mind, but it does seem to work. An observation by another interviewee doesn't flow exactly, but she predicted "hardly any jobs" will still be around much longer that don't require employees to be familiar with technology.

"There will be a war for talent," Moser went on. "You're going to see companies more and more do what we're doing: come alongside current employees and interns and train them, as well as pay for their education, because we have to. It's not extraordinary to have companies like mine doing that."

More than once or twice interviewees—not confident about what students tend to learn in school, be it in high school or afterward—talked about how businesses frequently prefer to handle the bulk of training themselves. Give employers smart people with reasonably strong technical aptitudes, and they'll take it from there, was the thought.

In talking about similar matters with economist King Banaian, I asked about skills young people need to be a machinist, mechanic, welder, and the like. "What I hear," he said, "from employers is 'I can train those people.'" Banaian also referred to a recruiting video sponsored by a welding company that announced, in effect, "We can teach you how to weld. We just need to know you're going to work hard, show up on time, and say 'please' and 'thank you.' If you can do that much for us, we'll teach you the rest of it. What we really need are people willing to work hard, because welding is hard work. Machining is hard work." The essential soldering of skills, hard and soft.

About a half hour later, I asked Banaian what it means for the economy and our country more broadly to have too few skilled workers. "I think we're going to see more capital investment. We're going to learn how to economize on labor. Therefore, we're going to get used to having fewer and fewer people in the workforce."

This is not an encouraging possibility. But it reinforces why people who do have the kinds of relatively scarce job skills we've been advocating are likely to do quite nicely in the main.

In much the same way "$30,000" cropped up several times when it came to college loans, so did the number "10" or "10 percent" or thereabouts come up regarding how much extra a company could do if it were adequately staffed.

Recall at the start of this chapter how the Manufacturing Institute and Deloitte estimated "average" manufacturers losing 11 percent of annual earnings because of talent shortages.

Also recall what Darlene Miller of Permac Industries said a few moments ago about having "our hands out all the time" and how she was eager to hire eight or ten more people if they were available.

According to David Siegel, executive director of BATC-Housing First Minnesota, "We're hearing across the association that a ten percent increase in business would not be sustainable right now because of lack of staffing." When it comes to building and remodeling homes, he said, it's taking four, five, or six months to do what you thought might take only two.

Stacey Stout, director of education and workforce development policy for the Minnesota Chamber of Commerce, upped the ante when she reported, "I met with members of the construction industry the other day, and they said that the lack of skilled people, or anybody truly interested in getting into the field, is limiting their businesses by 10 to 20 percent." There does seem to be another pattern.

Stout also noted, "Employers across our state and across all sectors are facing worker shortages," and then quickly added, "I didn't even say 'skilled' worker shortages." Her observation about unskilled workers is not surprising, especially given that many employers have greater confidence in their own ability to train employees than they have in the capacity of other places or institutions to do so. And then there is the reinforcing saw about how "on the job" training is the most effective kind.

Nonetheless, it's imperative not to lose sight of the kind of education and resulting skills in math and science that economist Eric A. Hanushek, among others, has stressed as pivotal to economic growth. The kinds of skills likely correlated, if roughly, with the amount of education or number of certificates or degrees a person has—but skills which sometimes don't correlate with amounts of education much at all, making many people without post–high school credentials fine and productive employees. Still, it would be a major mistake to assume that postsecondary certificates and degrees are anything other than consistently good and excellent things to earn and have, and not just for individuals, but the economy and wider society as well. As Hanushek has written:

> "Individuals with more measured cognitive skills systematically do better than those with less, and nations with a more skilled population grow faster than those with a less skilled population." Likewise, "There is now considerable evidence that cognitive skills measured by test scores are directly related to individual earnings, productivity, and economic growth."[13]

But if the relationship between cognitive skills and *individual* productivity and incomes is strong, the relationship between "measured labor force quality" and *national* economic growth is perhaps even stronger, as a "more skilled society" may lead to higher rates of invention, enable companies to introduce improved production methods, and lead to faster introduction of new technologies.[14]

A person's basic aptitude, not just what he or she studied in school or how strong their teachers were, has much to do with how well they learn things such as algebra and trigonometry, both of which are basic to various jobs we've been talking about. But even though my argument is that for many people, in many situations, less formal education is often just as good (if not better) than more formal education, it again would be a major mistake to take the assertion too far.

The focus of *Pathways to Prosperity*, published by the Harvard Graduate School of Education in 2011, is primarily on transitions between high school and what might, or might not, constitute postsecondary studies of some sort, including hanging out on old-style street corners. My focus is on transitions between high school and specific kinds of postsecondary institutions: four-year schools and two-year schools, as well as apprenticeships and military service. Nevertheless, *Pathways to Prosperity* (subtitled *Meeting the Challenge of Preparing Young Americans for the 21st Century*) was one of the more persuasive publications of its kind when I read it several years ago, and it remains so, especially since it contains a vivid critique of the "college-for-all" ethos, as in:

"[E]ducation reformers have mounted a sustained effort over the past two decades to raise standards, improve test-score performance, and promote 'college for all' as the primary pathway to success." This drive has had "many ameliorative effects." But after 20 years of strenuous and exceedingly expensive efforts, "the time has come for an honest assessment." While there have been modest gains, the movement's "bottom line measure of success is college completion. And on that score, we have still been unable to get more than 30 percent of young adults to earn a bachelor's degree by their mid-20s." And then the kicker: "'College for all' might be the mantra, but the hard reality is that fewer than one in three young people achieve the dream."

A few words about two more national reports, each offering plausible caveats to at least portions of my arguments so far.

Dismissed by Degrees: How Degree Inflation Is Undermining U.S. Competitiveness and Hurting America's Middle Class[15] challenges the idea that employers are as willing to hire men and women with credentials other than four-year degrees as I and others contend they are, never mind they're fully up to the job. Written principally by two Harvard Business School faculty, Joseph B. Fuller and Manjari Raman, and released in 2017, it notes that "Degree inflation—the rising demand for a four-year college degree for jobs that previously did not require one—is a substantive and widespread phenomenon that is making the U.S. labor market more inefficient." This pattern "hampers companies from finding the talent they need to grow and prosper and hinders Americans from accessing jobs that provide the basis for a decent standard of living."

A remarkable, which is not to say encouraging, statistic based on a review of 26 million job postings: In 2015, 67 percent of postings for "production supervisor" jobs asked for a four-year degree, while only 16 percent of then-employed production supervisors had one. "Our analysis," Fuller and Raman write, "indicates that more than 6 million jobs are currently at risk of degree inflation." Entirely unsurprisingly, CEOs cited in the report say that people with B.A.s don't necessarily perform better in middle-skills jobs than those with A.A.s, and often not as well.

How to reconcile these findings with evidence that well-trained men and women with less than baccalaureate degrees are in great demand in many places, often making more money than those with gaudier degrees? Squaring this circle is tough, other than by recognizing it's a big country with many different and differently accommodating job markets.

What industry, by the way, has the most jobs at risk of degree inflation? Not encouragingly again, manufacturing.

Briefly, one more complicating study calling, at minimum, for alertness and vigilance, this one having to do with automation:

Jobs Lost, Jobs Gained: Workforce Transitions in a Time of Automation[16] is a study by McKinsey & Company, released also in 2017, that examines work around the world "that can be automated through 2030 and jobs that may be created in the same period." McKinsey concludes, "Even if there is enough work to ensure full employment by 2030, major transitions lie ahead that could match and even exceed the scale of historical shifts out of agriculture and manufacturing." Only a year later it was hard to know what kind of comfort to take when former Secretary of State George P. Shultz wrote of the "sophisticated use of robotics" laboring alongside "human colleagues."[17]

McKinsey's "scenarios" suggest that by 2030, somewhere between 75 million and 375 million workers, which will be 3 to 14 percent of the worldwide workforce, will "need to switch occupational categories." And then a moment later, getting closer to the pertinent heart, "Income polarization could continue in the United States and other advanced economies, where demand for high-wage occupations may grow the most while *middle-wage occupations decline*—assuming current wage structures persist (emphasis supplied)." If it lifts any spirits, I learned from my time in state government that economic forecasts are hardly ever right, though McKinsey does give itself a lot of wiggle room.

There is a risk of seeming to make too little of what may wind up being an enormous problem for many people in the United States and elsewhere: a future in which they truly won't fit because of inadequate or wrong skills. I'm not suggesting or predicting this, in fact, will be the case, as I usually live on the reasonably optimistic side of such ledgers. But it takes only one conversation over lunch (which I just had) with a friend who has a particularly expansive and sober grasp of artificial intelligence to envision half-full glasses turning into half-empty leaking ones. Or at least until a drink at dinner replenishes.

Or until one perhaps retrieves hope by reading a very good countervailing essay by Oren Cass of the Manhattan Institute, "Is Technology Destroying the Labor Market?"[18] "If automation," he writes, "were rendering workers obsolete, we would see the evidence in rising productivity, major capital investments, and a shift in the ratio of production workers to managerial workers. None of these things has occurred. If technology could render workers obsolete, the radical advancements of past generations should have done it. They did not. If this time is different," Cass concludes, "we should find evidence that a large share of current workers are uniquely vulnerable to the particular set of technologies on the horizon. We do not."

Let's begin to conclude the chapter by getting a sense of additional educational and training programs around the country in which business leaders are integrally at the table and need to be. Stacey Stout of the Minnesota Chamber of Commerce told me of the Minnesota Chamber's Business Education Networks, which started as a pilot program in Winona, in the southeastern corner of the state along the Mississippi River, with an aim of narrowing skills gaps by better connecting employers with both high school and college students as well as with higher education institutions and workforce training activities.

Business Education Networks have expanded to six other locations across Minnesota. Also included in the initiative is Teacher in the Workplace, a program in which high school teachers in the area participate in one-week, paid summer immersion programs at area manufacturing companies. According to Stout, one of the virtues of the program is that science, math, industrial tech, and other teachers come away with a better sense of what those competencies "look like in application." In talking about the world within the walls of a local manufacturer, a shop teacher said afterward, "There's a lot more here than I thought." Especially given how high school counselors generally know very little about manufacturing as a career, one would expect both teachers and students to benefit from programs like this.

As was the case in chapter 3, I'm indebted to my American Experiment colleague Katherine Kersten for compiling and describing the next three initiatives, among others.[19]

CareerWise Colorado, a nonprofit, public-private partnership, aims at "building the middle class by closing the skills gap through experiential learning." It assists employers in setting up three-year, paid apprenticeships in high-tech fields such as advanced manufacturing and information technology. Participating students combine two or three days of on-the-job training with two or three days of classroom learning. They also learn soft skills in a "professionalism boot camp." A third year of apprenticeship training after high school prepares them to start working immediately or to go on and complete a two-year or four-year degree. One goal of CareerWise Colorado is to have 20,000 young people in apprenticeships by 2027. That would represent about 10 percent of the state's high school juniors and seniors.

Ivy Tech Community College, with 45 campuses throughout Indiana, is the single-largest accredited statewide community college system in the United States. It's a national leader in coordinating academic programs with on-the-job training to "ensure that experiential learning is valued and can lead to an academic certificate or degree." A main goal is making certain that the sprawling institution offers exactly what employers need and that all credentials are "stackable" in the sense that they can be applied to more advanced certificates or degrees.

For instance, Ivy Tech collaborates with unions to offer an associate of applied science degree, which incorporates on-the-job training required for a journeyman's card with the general education courses required for an associate's degree. It's available to workers in 15 trades, including bricklayers, electricians, and ironworkers. Ivy Tech also offers a similar interdisciplinary associate's degree in advanced manufacturing.

KY FAME (Kentucky Federation for Advanced Manufacturing Education) was started in 2008 by a "handful of frustrated employers who resolved to 'grow their own talent.'" The employers joined with a nearby technical college to design a two-year advanced manufacturing technician (AMT) program to meet what was called their "greatest skill need." Students in the dual-track apprenticeship program include recent high school graduates as well as veterans and full-time workers seeking to upgrade their skills and career prospects.

Students spend two days a week in college classes and work for their employer-sponsor three days a week. Courses include academic subjects such as math and English, technical subjects such as welding and pneumatics, and soft skills such as timeliness and teamwork. Graduates wind up with an industry-recognized associate of applied science degree, with most finishing debt free, as employers generally assume all costs while students are working for them.

A chapter titled "Potential Economic Detours" can suggest as broad an expanse of questions as one chooses to draw. For our purposes, critical concerns have been confined principally to matters of education and training. Up next is a chapter on "Potential Social Detours," which may be viewed as less lasered, dealing as it does with matters of race, class, mobility, marriage, and their unwieldy like.

NOTES

1. Jason A. Tyszko, Gardner A. Carrick, and Robert G. Sheets, "Quality Pathways: Employer Leadership in Earn & Learn Opportunities," U.S. Chamber of Commerce Foundation and Manufacturing Institute, 2018.

2. https://www.pmpa.org/careers/right-skills-now.

3. "Baby Boomers Retire," Pew Research Center, December 29, 2010.

4. *The Skills Gap in U.S. Manufacturing 2015 and Beyond*, sponsored by The Manufacturing Institute and Deloitte, 2015.

5. Deloitte analysis based on data from the U.S. Bureau of Labor Statistics as well as a Gallup survey.

6. Ibid.

7. *Out of Inventory: Skills Shortage Threatens Growth for US Manufacturing*. Accenture 2014 Manufacturing Skills and Training Study.

8. "Companies Losing Money to the Skills Gap," according to CareerBuilder Study, March 2014.

9. *Rising Above the Gathering Storm: Energizing and Employing America for a Brighter Economic Future*, National Academies, 2005.

10. *Rising Above the Gathering Storm, Revisited: Rapidly Approaching Category 5*, National Academies, 2010.

11. World Economic Forum, *The Global Competitiveness Report 2009–2010*.

12. http://www.oecd.org/dataoecd/41/25/43636332.pdf.

13. Eric A. Hanushek, "The Economic Value of Education and Cognitive Skills," in *Handbook of Education Policy Research*, Barbara Schneider and David N. Plank, eds. (New York: Routledge, 2009), pp. 39–56.

14. For a fuller discussion regarding points like these, see Mitch Pearlstein, *From Family Collapse to America's Decline: The Educational, Economic, and Social Costs of Family Fragmentation* (Lanham, MD: Rowman & Littlefield, 2011), chapter 4.

15. Joseph B. Fuller, Manjari Raman, et al., *Dismissed by Degrees: How Degree Inflation Is Undermining U.S. Competitiveness and Hurting America's Middle Class*, Accenture, Grads of Life, Harvard Business School, October 2017.

16. *Jobs Lost, Jobs Gained: Workforce Transitions in a Time of Automation*, McKinsey & Company, December 2017.

17. George P. Shultz, "America Can Ride the 21st Century's Waves of Change," *Wall Street Journal*, June 28, 2018.

18. Oren Cass, "Is Technology Destroying the Labor Market?" *City Journal*, Spring 2018.

19. Katherine Kersten, "Why It's Time to Hit Reset on 'Vocational' Education," *Thinking Minnesota*, Center of the American Experiment, Golden Valley, MN, Spring 2018, pp. 22–25.

Chapter 6

Potential Social Detours

Two complicating issues addressed in this chapter are particularly intricate societally. (I'm trying to avoid the clichéd "socially sensitive.") One issue focuses on matters of *marriage* and class, the other on matters of *race* and class. In each instance, little has been heard about how they interweave with educational options as specifically understood and advanced in this book. To get going, here are two questions regarding marriage, class, and the less-traveled educational paths we've been talking about. We'll deal with questions of race and class later in the chapter.

Big question: Will women with four-year and graduate degrees be as interested in becoming seriously involved with highly skilled and well-paid men in the trades, as they customarily are with highly skilled and well-paid men who have B.A.s and M.B.A.s? Bluntly put, will such women be matrimonially uninterested in men who wear uniforms at work instead of suits and ties? Or, more ecumenically, will significant differences in educational backgrounds pose no great problem?

I had a conversation several years ago with one of my adult stepsons in which we wound up talking about his circle of friends. I was intrigued by how everyone he described sounded as if they had at least a bachelor's degree, except for one friend who sounded blue collar. Being sociologically intrigued by how my stepson and the rest of the gang related to him and vice versa, I was quickly informed that all was fine, no sweat, what's the big deal? Which left me sounding like King Pomposity in our shared circle of family.

But no matter how questions like mine might come across, the issue I raised is real and germane. This is the case, given growing suggestions that many young men would be better off if they seriously considered educational options routinely viewed as less prestigious than a baccalaureate—at the very same time many young women presumably view, no better than tepidly, the idea of marrying men with less-esteemed educations and careers than they have. Whatever else their wedding dreams might be, and not to be unkind, a key one for many young women as well as young men is to wind up in an assortative marriage; a union where women and men of roughly similar educational backgrounds find each other, quite likely after purposefully looking.

Robert D. Putnam has written about the segregating aspects of assortative mating, as in his well-attended-to 2015 book, *Our Kids: The American Dream in Crisis*.[1] Here's a key passage: "In the second half of the [twentieth] century, Americans increasingly married people with educational backgrounds similar to their own, with the most educated especially likely to marry one another. In other words, as the gap between rich and poor narrowed in the first half of the twentieth century, more and more Romeos and Juliets jumped across, but as the economic and educational gulf has widened in more recent decades, fewer and fewer people are finding partners on the other side."[2]

In terms of how this dynamic broadly impinges on matters of social class, and in a cross between an article and a blog, psychologist Nicholas Zill pondered the question: "Does the 'Marriage of Equals' Exacerbate Educational Inequality?"[3] Drawing on data from a major longitudinal study conducted by the U.S. Department of Education,[4] he persuasively answers, "Yes," it does. This is important, but my interest at this stage is less on the ways assortative marriage contributes to educational and, hence, economic inequality nationally, but rather on how it plays out in individual lives. For instance, I assume more young men and young women with undergraduate and graduate degrees harbor hopes of settling down (rudely for effect again) with their "equals" rather than fantasize about meeting the tradesman or tradeswoman of their dreams. We will return to impulses like these.

The idea that Americans are divided from each other every which way, as argued by Zill, Putnam, and many others,[5] has reached the level of cliché. No question, we are divvied in many respects, more so than often in the past. But it's also clear, at least to me, that we regularly get along better with each other than often assumed, which is no small matter. Nevertheless, the central question before us, in the context of the book, has less to do with any kind of cohering civility than with the kinds of differences keeping individuals firmly apart. More specifically in this instance, I'm interested in men and women who, save for differences in education and subsequent careers, might otherwise have seen each other as possible spouses.

Thinking of my own social life, much of it radiates from St. George's Episcopal Church in St. Louis Park, Minnesota, where my wife, the Rev. Diane Darby McGowan, is the deacon. Sometimes I know exactly how much formal education a parishioner has, yet in most cases I can only guess. Beyond, St. George's is a *community* where differences of many sorts are blurred rather than accentuated. Such is one of the virtues of institutional religion, or at least it should be.

But are not young people attending religious services at measurably lower rates than their elders did when they were much younger, as well as less frequently than older men and women are now? And don't single people attend church less frequently than married people? Both true, meaning great numbers of millennials and other non-ancients are losing out on opportunities to nourish friendships, and perhaps romances, where the societally attached prestige of their credentials (or lack thereof) is of less distinguishing importance than it might be the other six days of the week.[6] (To clear up any head-scratching, yes, I'm Jewish, but I also answer to "Senior Auxiliary Member of St. George's, Self-Appointed.")

As has been the case throughout the book, the main frames of the last few pages have been young people needing to decide, as they're graduating from high school, whether to attend a four-year college or perhaps a community college. Or perhaps sign up for a stint in the military, participate in an apprenticeship, or seek a certificate. Also posed, albeit quickly, have been questions about young men whose parallel life-shaping decisions are between an A.A.S. and no more formal education at all, or between a certificate program and, again, no more formal education at all. In instances like this, a less-than-four-year degree, as opposed to nothing beyond high school, presumably would *increase* rather than diminish a young man's chances of finding a wife, if that, in fact, was his aim (and hers).

Suffice it to say, not everyone I interviewed saw the mating dance of men and women with sizably different educational backgrounds as potentially difficult as I do. A major reason for their confidence, as at least one respondent put it, is that "money talks." They contended that many men with two-year degrees in the trades and other fields would continue making more money than many women with four-year degrees and higher, as well as more money than many men with B.A.s and additional degrees, and that these financial facts of life will lead to more "mixed" marriages of a socioeconomic sort. The following are some of those arguments.

The last time we heard from Darlene Miller, owner of Permac Industries, was in chapter 5, when she talked about how she would like to hire eight or ten more good people if she could find them. This time, she assured that she has "many friends who are professional women who are married to men in the trades. They're great relationships. It all comes back to how it takes intelligence to do both kinds of jobs. You might not think my employees have an interest in the theater or in politics. But it's totally the opposite. I hear it every day in their conversation. There are a lot of misconceptions."

The last time we heard from Sandra Kresbach, executive director of the American Technical Education Association, was in chapter 4, when she talked about the prudence of acquiring a certificate as a backup plan if the rest of a person's education and career are not in sync. In this instance, and after a preamble not unlike the one at the top of this chapter, I asked her how often people with certificates and two-year degrees wind up in marriages and social circles where there are a lot of people with M.B.A.s.

"First of all," she said, "money talks." Whatever differences might exist, she said, tend to fade. And to the extent one partner has college debt, "that's not all that attractive" to the other.

Kresbach, who has a doctorate, went on to note how she and her husband belong to a golf club that has "lots of entrepreneurs. Many of them have degrees, but some probably don't." She added that when she and her husband got married, he had completed three, not four, years of college, and it took a while for him to get his bachelor's degree, as Vietnam interfered. "I'm certainly not saying, don't ever get a four-year degree. I'm saying, even if you get it 15 years later, you have it."

The last time we heard from David Siegel, executive director of the Builders Association of the Twin Cities, was in chapter 5, when he spoke of having a hard time hiring enough qualified people. As for the subject at hand, and in the spirit of "money talks," he said, "I think it depends on whether she perceives he's going to be able to make some dough. And if she thinks he can make some good money in this business, I don't think it's going to matter" if he has less education than she does, and she has a fancier title than he has. "I think it's a question of whether she understands that this guy, who's a plumber, is going to yank down a hundred G's a year, or 90 or 80, and have a pretty good life. I think it comes down to, 'Are we going to have a pretty good life together financially?'"

With all these examples, keep in mind that people in the trades with a year or two of postsecondary education often make more money than people with multiples of that amount of college.

The last time we heard from Rassoul Dastmozd, president of Saint Paul College, was in chapter 3, when he argued for exposing young people to non-four-year degrees and careers as early as fourth grade. In talking about the kinds of socioeconomically mixed marriages I had raised, he argued, "First of all, my friend, love is blind. This country never would have fathomed a person of the Jewish faith marrying a Christian or a Muslim. Or a white person marrying an African American. Or a person from a rich banking family marrying someone in a service industry. But we've proven it all exists. They're not anomalies anymore. To me, as this country becomes more diverse, as we have more diversity of occupations, we will see more of the marriages you're talking about." Of note, Dastmozd is originally from Iran.

Finally, there is Darlynn Benjamin, from whom we haven't yet heard but will as we continue, who used to work for Minnesota Congressman Keith

Ellison. She asked, "What's the difference between a two-year-degree person marrying a four-year-degree person and trying to figure out life, compared to a black person and a white person getting together and trying to figure out life? There are pressures within the marriage, societal pressures, cultural differences. I like to do things *this* way; you like to do things *that* way."

Of note, Darlynn Benjamin is African American, as is her husband Lindsay, the program manager who rhapsodized about driving 18-wheelers when we last heard from him in chapter 3. This time he suggested in a joint interview with Darlynn how differences in pronouncing "potato" and "tomato" (with a hard or soft "a") were metaphors for the kinds of differences expanded on by his wife. He might have said this glibly, but it works.

I asked Darlynn and Lindsay if I possibly was making too much of the issue. Would men, in fact, find it harder to build lives with women if proportionately growing numbers of males had two-year degrees and less, while constant or growing numbers of females had four-year degrees and perhaps more? To which Lindsay said, "It's a possibility, but it's less of an issue than it was, and I hope it will be an even smaller issue in the future. Most of the women I work with likely make more money than their husbands. If you meet someone you're compatible with, but the two of you do different things, say one of you is a neurosurgeon and the other is a bus driver, you both go to work in a uniform, right?"

Not exactly, as that comment was wholly glib. But Lindsay was wholly right when he said, "God has a sense of humor" about things like this.

Let's move to a few comments by interviewees that better align with my more hesitant views about men and women from different educational and occupational worlds finding each other and then, even more importantly, staying together. One of the more striking things said by any respondent in this regard was by King Banaian, dean of the School of Public Affairs of St. Cloud State University in Minnesota. "I mentioned my first wife, who's deceased," he said. "She never went to college. We were fine through my time as an undergraduate, but she had no capacity to understand much of what was going on in my life when I was in graduate school. We became estranged and eventually divorced."

Twice previously in the book I've mentioned an invaluable summer roundtable conversation with five young women, all of whom were entering their sophomore year at five excellent universities across the country. One topic that we talked about that I've not yet cited was whether they could ever see themselves marrying a man with significantly less education than the five of them are on early schedule to get. With all due respect, it was hard to miss their uncomfortableness and to-and-froing. Here are comments by all five of the women.[7]

First interviewee: "I would say I would be much less likely to marry someone without a college degree. I'm not into status that way, but I would be less likely to think we would be intellectually similar. Now, if I met a plumber who was intellectually stimulating, that would be fine. But in general, I would have less in common with people without a college degree, and so I would be more likely to marry someone who does have one. I'm also just more likely to interact with people with college degrees, meaning that's where I'm likely to meet a spouse."

Second interviewee: "I think I would probably be more likely to marry someone with a college degree. Not necessarily because of anything intellectual, but simply because I'll be interacting with them at school."

I followed up by asking, "So let's say you've finished school, and you're a full-fledged architect. You're 30, you're doing well, and you meet a guy you really like but he's a carpenter."

"I might be less inclined to know him well. I would like to say that wouldn't be the case, but . . ." And her voice faded.

Third interviewee: "I agree with the first two women when they spoke about interaction. I'm just more likely to meet someone who has a college degree, or will be introduced to him by someone who's going to college, or something like that. But it would really depend on who he is. I don't think I would rule people out because they don't have a college degree, because there could be a lot more to someone's story."

I upped the ante: "Let's say you don't just have a bachelor's degree, but a Ph.D., or at least a master's. You're now two or three levels above. Would that change the situation at all?"

"I don't know. Maybe, maybe not. But if they had a stable job and hadn't ruled out college because they didn't want to learn anything, but because they had other opportunities, I feel like then I would be fine with that."

This answer was influenced by the fact that she was working in retail for a man she appeared to respect but who did not have a college degree, though he had taken community college courses.

Fourth interviewee: "I agree with everyone about the practical difficulties of interacting with people without a degree, but there also is a little bit of prejudice on my part because ambition is always an attractive thing for me. I feel that people who don't pursue a four-year degree are viewed as less ambitious, but it's probably a case-by-case thing. If it's not just a matter of their not wanting to go to college but having an alternative they are passionate about and wanted to pursue, I think I would probably be fine with that. I don't think it would ever be a deal breaker with me, even if I had a Ph.D. and the person is right. But I probably would be less likely to give them as much of a chance because of my assumptions, unfortunately."

Fifth interviewee: "It's kind of tricky with nursing school, since it's mostly girls. But my aunt is a nurse, and she married a carpenter who didn't go to college, and they're happy. They had ten kids, and I could see they were fine and that everyone was happy. I don't think I would rule someone completely out just because he was a carpenter or a plumber. But I would hope that whoever I marry would have a stable job so we could be financially okay and hopefully get to travel and own a house."

Perfectly understandable comments such as these recall the article by Nicholas Zill, cited at the top of the chapter, about whether the marriage of educational equals worsens educational inequality. Yes, it does, he wrote. But on the plus side, "it also contributes to educational excellence. Young people of exceptional accomplishment, such as winners of the Intel Science Talent Search, child prodigies in music and the visual arts, or youthful creators of new cell phone apps and video games often have mothers and fathers who both have above-average levels of education, talent, and accomplishment."

The study he focused on doesn't include community college degrees or occupational certificates among its educational levels but rather looks at parental categories such as "Neither finished H.S.," "One finished H.S.," "Both finished H.S.," "One had some college," "Both had some college," all the way to "Both have graduate degrees."

Well-educated young women and young men, I would argue, usually grasp how their eventual children will do better educationally and economically (to retrieve an offensive saw for effect) if they refrain from marrying "beneath their station." They implicitly recognize that children born of two parents each with a master's, will do better than boys and girls (if only modestly and always on average) born to parents with a master's and two-year diploma. This may sound cold, but it's also unremarkable. As is the way fewer physicians, I'm guessing, marry their receptionists. If, in fact, this is the case, there are several reasons, including the emergence of less-personal group practices, not to mention the explosion of female doctors and the increasing number of male receptionists. But also involved, I would argue, are the patterns and dictates of associative marriage.

We met sisters Carlita, Kaylee, and Kerry, brother Ryan, and Kaylee's husband Josh in chapter 4, talking about their college debts, some of which were huge. This chapter, we have the good fortune of hearing again from Carlita, with an intriguing recommendation at the intersection of debt and marriage. We were talking about the difficulties of finding spouses when Ryan said something about dating services. This prompted Carlita to propose a new online profile question, "How much debt do you have?" I'm guessing she said this in much the same glib way Lindsay talked about potatoes and tomatoes. Then again, maybe not.

Yet either way, a serious question: Starting with an understanding that some people are not perfectly honest in filling out questionnaires, do you think a man who may not otherwise come across as particularly attractive or impressive can quickly become appealing in the eyes of some women if his profile announces he is free of all or almost all college debt? How often do you think this might happen, if it happened at all? Either way, what might it say about the power of college debt to shape or misshape lives?

Nathaniel Elifson and Matthew Nickolay graduated a couple of years ago from Hope Academy, a "high quality Christ-centered" school that is situated in a low-income Minneapolis neighborhood and uses a "a rigorous Classical curriculum throughout our K–12 program." When we spoke, Nate was a welding student at Minneapolis Community and Technical College, and Matthew was a two-year HVAC student at Dunwoody College. We will hear next chapter about why they picked the majors and careers they did and the satisfaction they derive from them. But for now, let's listen to Nate, who was responding to my argument that large numbers of women holding at least four-year degrees do not see men holding less-celebrated credentials as prime candidates for marriage.

"I would agree with your premise," he started. "I've been concerned that maybe a woman I'm interested in marrying would not want to marry me based on what I do. I guess I've developed an attitude of, 'Well, if she can't appreciate me for who I am as a man, then she's definitely not the one for me.' I've always believed that if you love what you do, and you're willing to do it every day for the rest of your life, then you're going to be a happier person. And if a woman can't accept that because I work with machines that get my hands greasy, and I get dirt under my nails, she's definitely not someone I could truly love."

For the only time in any of the interviews, I talked of an interviewee "entwined" in things Christian, with the people he hangs out with and the people he might wind up marrying also part of that world.

This was near the end our conversation, and I asked if either wanted to add anything. Matthew didn't but Nate did.

"I go to the Hope Community Church downtown. Great church, I really enjoy it, and there are many more women than men in the pews on Sundays. I believe there are lots more Christian women looking to get married than there are Christian men. My older sister calls it the 'Christian Discount.'"

"Oh my, that's good," I said laughing.

"So I'm not really too worried about my odds of getting married."

An apt segue to matters of race and class is how African American women are earning more academic and professional degrees than African American men and how those disparities are complicating and constraining their marital prospects. One insightful place to look is a 2011 book by Ralph Richard

Banks, a Stanford law professor, with the telling title *Is Marriage for White People?*

Early on, Banks writes that while the decline in marriage among African Americans is especially severe among the poor, it's also going on among professionals. "Black women of all socioeconomic classes remain single in part because the ranks of black men have been decimated by incarceration, educational failure, and economic disadvantage. . . . As a result, college-educated black women are more likely than college-educated women of other races to remain unmarried or to wed a less-educated man who earns less than they do."[8]

While the situation Banks describes is an "apt segue," it's far from perfect, as the men I'm writing about are neither now, nor will they likely wind up being, incarcerated or in the other tough situations he writes about. The alternative educational and career paths I'm advocating lead to solid middle-class lives, not impoverished or severely damaged ones. The potential connection, however, that does exist is the way in which great numbers of black women either never marry, or if they do, enter marriages that may (or may not) prove less satisfying and successful for reasons of educational and/or occupational distance within their unions. Divorces are the result of a lot of things, but it's telling and disturbing that Banks reports how "black spouses are, by some estimates, nearly twice as likely as their white counterparts to divorce."[9]

Nevertheless, it wasn't only marriage that first got me thinking about how non-four-year degree programs related to matters of race and class. It also was how low-income kids and kids of color in elementary schools—inner-city schools, perhaps in particular—are often called "scholars" by teachers and principals. How, I wondered, does referring to boys and girls so loftily fit with urging young people to at least consider technical and other alternative routes; paths in which intelligence is essential, but which generally are not described as "scholarly"? Might such suggestions undercut the very notion of "scholarly"? How, in short, might suggestions in the book be received, especially by parents and grandparents who view vocational education as dead-end tracking? Or even shorter, might I be making too much out of simply sweet salutations?

I also asked myself, if the kinds of non-four-year options described in these pages are as strong as I say they are, why wouldn't they be just as career-enhancing for poor kids as more middle-class ones? And if that were the case, as it is, wouldn't downplaying what apprenticeships, stints in the military, A.A. degrees, and certificates can do for them, out of fear of kindling bad memories of bad shop classes constitute a denial of opportunity and no favor or respect at all? Yes, it would.

Janet L. Yellen, former chair of the Federal Reserve Board, acknowledged in a 2017 speech that "for some time, vocational education had fallen out of favor or was in decline in the United States, as it was associated with the deleterious practice of 'tracking' less-advantaged students that denied them the opportunity for the best education."[10] Or, as vividly put by Darlynn Benjamin, older conceptions of vocational education effectively "redlined" the futures of many low-income students and students of color.

A reverberation of that insulting and stifling history played out in an interview with two African American leaders when I used the term "trade schools." I use the term only sporadically, not that I've thought of it as a pejorative, but I did use it during a conversation with the husband and wife team of Don and Sondra Samuels, and it struck a nerve. Don was quick to respond: Before he could credibly recommend such institutions, he said, to "people whose biggest challenge is lack of respect, the respectability of trade schools needs to be restored." He likewise made it clear during our conversation that the same requirement applied to what he saw as other suspect, vocationally oriented institutions and programs.

In this dispirit, a recent National Public Radio story spoke of how views like this, grounded in historically harsh perceptions, "fuel the worry that if students are urged as early as the seventh grade to consider the trades, low-income, first-generation, and ethnic and racial minority high school students will be channeled into blue-collar jobs while wealthier and white classmates are pushed by their parents to get bachelor's degrees."[11]

Don, whose main background is in business, is executive director of a Twin Cities nonprofit and a former candidate for mayor of Minneapolis as well as a former member of the Minneapolis Board of Education. He and his wife, Sondra, are also good friends of mine. Immediately after he said what he did about trade schools, Sondra began talking about what it's taking to create a "college-going culture in North Minneapolis," where she is president and CEO of the Northside Achievement Zone (NAZ), a "wraparound framework that effectively supports low-income children of color so that they will graduate from high school prepared for college." NAZ is in the spirit of the Harlem Children's Zone, created by the celebrated Geoffrey Canada.

At the very same time I'm not-so-subtly trying to get likely college-going young people to consider non-four-year routes, Sondra and her NAZ colleagues are subtly trying to get local parents to think explicitly for the first time about four-year degrees for their children. "We don't have a college-going culture right now," she said, "for low-income folks in Minneapolis. If anyone goes anywhere after high school, it's to get a certificate or a trade. We're trying to solve the problem, 'How do we create a culture of college-going achievement?'"

To this end, NAZ, with the help of Target Corporation, pulled together "about nine parents, all moms, and we asked them a series of non-leading questions," Sondra said. "We just had a conversation with them. Everybody was low-income with one or two of them white. What we heard was that 'college is not all that.' Not high praise. They said they knew some people who graduated from college, and they're crazy, or they don't have a job. 'So, if my daughter wants to be a beautician, or anything like that, that's fine with me,' they said. It was like, 'Maybe they go, maybe they don't, as long as they're happy.' And what they mean by 'happy' is that their children can take care of themselves, they're emotionally and financially okay, and they do a little better than their parents. That's what we were getting: 'Whatever they want to do,' but it wasn't college."

Given this context, Sondra and her colleagues decided to focus on the idea of "postsecondary," rather than "college" as such, and stress how "these opportunities are pathways to happiness," being sure to "get college squarely in the mix because the other options already are."

Don spoke with similar nuance in talking about how it wasn't long ago when "bright, young African Americans were forced to work with their hands because they couldn't get other opportunities." Think of Pullman porters, he said. "They often had the capacity to lead at the highest levels but were still performing with their hands. These men were the cream of the crop of the black community, and for many years they were the deacons in our churches, they were the trustees, they were the community leaders. But then their children often wound up saying, 'My dad was a brilliant man, but they wouldn't let him do other things. And not only that, they tried to do that to me, too.' And they're like, 'No more. No more.' That's the black middle class."

In the months after interviewing the Samuelses, I mentioned what Don had said about trade schools to several other interviewees. It's fair to say they were of a different mind. Houston White, for instance, whom we met in chapter 3, is the entrepreneurial owner of H. White's Men's Room, a North Minneapolis barbershop (and much more) in the important and storied tradition of African American barbershops. "I went to a trade school," he said. "It's an old southern thing. People would always say 'get a trade' and that was linked to the tradition of being self-sufficient. The word 'trade' carries a lot of valor, as does the name 'trade school.' It's a badge of honor to say you have a trade." Houston grew up in Mississippi.

In fairness to Don, his problem was with the term *trade schools*, not the trades themselves, and perhaps I'm being a bit unfair by dwelling on the name. But I've cited what he and Houston had to say, as their respective comments speak to the often emotionally drenched subtleties of language in all of this and the care required in its use.

Racially rooted hesitations and opposition can lead to a lack of interest, never mind enthusiasm, in the kinds of educational and career options advocated in this book. Leading, in turn, to sad irony, as such options can be particularly helpful to exactly the people who have been disrespected and educationally shortchanged. Or in entirely nonracial terms, the kinds of pathways I'm talking about apply to students of all backgrounds, with all kinds of grades and test scores. But they apply especially to young people who have not had the best, or most enjoyable, or most profitable of times in school.

No other interviewees reacted to any language I used in the same way Don and Sondra did. Several people I interviewed, in fact, had positive, if qualified, things to say about what might be thought of as benign, latter-day tracking. Rassoul Dastmozd, president of the two-year Saint Paul College, was one of them:

"Let's be intentional. Let's get away from this labeling, 'Oh, we're tracking students.' There is nothing wrong with providing pathways for students past fifth grade, as long as there is an opportunity for them to get a four-year applied degree. Pathways like this exist. They exist in Germany."

Writing in the *Wall Street Journal*, the Manhattan Institute's Oren Cass suggested a variation when he wrote that while the refusal to track is an egalitarian impulse, the "insistence on treating everyone equally in high school harms students for whom the college track is not appropriate. It deprives them of schooling that could be more valuable and abandons them after graduation ill-prepared for work."[12]

An interviewee, Dave Kornecki, was quick to point out we already embrace tracking. "It's called college," he said. And another, Checker Finn, spoke similarly about "shunting" kids off to college.

If I were to guess, Finn isn't fond of words like "track" and "tracking," but he approvingly pointed out—rightly so—how advocates and writers are using "pathways" as a rough but effectively cleansed alternative. Recall, for example, the excellent Harvard report, *Pathways to Prosperity*,[13] a title much more felicitous than *Tracks to Prosperity*. As for the *concept* of tracking, not just the word, Finn argued that vocational education withered partly because it did, in fact, smack of segregation and illiberal practices, as poor kids and black and brown kids were sent to shop classes while white and Asian kids would do college prep, and that it did, indeed, constitute an "evil thing." And as with Dastmozd, he emphasized the pivotal importance of students being able to change paths if they chose.

When it comes to Career and Technical Education (CTE), Finn said, "You should always be able to change paths if you want to." Of a piece with all this, Anthony Carnevale of the Georgetown University Center on Education and the Workforce was asked in 2013 how to prevent CTE "from becoming a ghettoized path." To which he assured, CTE "isn't a path away from college," as it's "simply another way to get there."[14]

What about the idea of referring to children as "scholars"? What about addressing five-year-old and six-year-old kids in ways graduate students only dream about? I have no problem with it, and neither did any interviewees. "Calling somebody a scholar," one educator said effusively, "helps them understand their locus of control and self-efficacy and helps them develop the grit and resilience to survive the ups and downs they will encounter." Another interviewee said, "You would hope parents treat their children in scholarly ways." But the most interesting thing said was by Frank Forsberg, the former United Way official we heard from in chapter 3, whose father had started off as a dishwasher but wound up owning bakeries.

Calling children "scholars," he said, is very useful, especially when starting in kindergarten or first or second grade. But, he added intriguingly, "I'm not certain about its impact on the child, as I'm thinking more about its impact on all the adults surrounding the child." He said he found calling children scholars a "useful tool to challenge people, disproportionately white adults working in neighborhoods of color, to think about the children they're teaching or supporting as potential scholars. Because otherwise their implicit bias may get in the way of their holding expectations for those boys and girls as high as they have for their own."

I pushed and asked if he thought implicit bias was, in fact, a big problem.

"I think implicit bias is real, and I think it's serious. It's part of the barriers that get in the way of young children of color succeeding."

Several other topics which fall neatly under the heading "Potential Social Detours" fit just as well under "Conclusion," and we'll save them for that last chapter. They include keenly important matters of inequality and mobility, leaving two quick items to finish this chapter.

How much is postsecondary education valued by Americans, especially those of color?[15] A 2014 Gallup poll found that Hispanics and blacks are more likely than whites to say that having a college education leads to a better quality of life and agree that more Americans should earn a degree. While 56 percent of whites said it is very important to increase the proportion of Americans with some form of a college degree, 72 percent of Hispanics and 73 percent of blacks felt the same way. Note that these results were not just for four-year institutions, but for "some form of a college degree" or "professional certificate." Good survey construction.

Last item: Our main focus has been on high school students and what they might do after graduation. But, again, what about young people who drop out of high school? What about their prospects? They can be promising, as the United States is not just a land of opportunity but one of second and third chances.

Difficult though it may be, people who drop out can earn a GED and then take advantage of most of the paths discussed here, including pursuit of a four-year degree, if that is their dream. If we were to consider men particularly, I can't think of anything that can make them more marriageable in the eyes of women than earning a degree (whatever kind it might be) or earning a certificate (in whatever field it might be) or learning a trade in the military (out of the shiploads offered). I also can't think of routes more likely to help them become good fathers to their children and good husbands to their wives.

NOTES

1. Robert D. Putnam, *Our Kids: The American Dream in Crisis* (New York: Simon & Schuster, 2015).
2. Ibid, p. 40.
3. Nicholas Zill, "Does the 'Marriage of Equals' Exacerbate Educational Inequality?" Institute for Family Studies, March 31, 2016.
4. Known as ECLS-K, it was (in Zill's words) "a national survey of some 19,000 kindergarten pupils and their parents, schools, and teachers. More than 6,000 children in the original sample were followed from the start of kindergarten to the end of eighth grade. The study collected information from the resident parent about the educational attainment of biological fathers and mothers who were no longer living with the child."
5. For example, see Bill Bishop, *The Big Sort: Why the Clustering of Like-Minded America Is Tearing Us Apart* (New York: Houghton Mifflin Harcourt, 2008).
6. See, for example, Robert D. Putnam and David E. Campbell, *American Grace: How Religion Divides and Unites Us* (New York: Simon & Schuster, 2010); and W. Bradford Wilcox and Nicholas H. Wolfinger, *Soul Mates: Religion, Sex, Love, and Marriage among African Americans and Latinos* (New York: Oxford, 2016).
7. It's not as if anyone said anything terrible or terribly embarrassing, but I'm just more comfortable not using their names.
8. Ralph Richard Banks, *Is Marriage for White People?* (New York: Plume, 2011).
9. Ibid., p. 8.
10. Janet L. Yellen, "Addressing Workforce Development Challenges in Low-Income Communities," National Community Reinvestment Coalition, March 28, 2017.
11. Ashley Gross and Jon Marcus, "High-Paying Trade Jobs Sit Empty, While High School Grads Line Up for University," NPR News, April 25, 2018.
12. Oren Cass, "Not Everyone Should Go to College," *Wall Street Journal*, May 18, 2018.
13. *Pathways to Prosperity: Meeting the Challenge of Preparing Young Americans for the 21st Century*, Harvard Graduate School of Education, February 2011.
14. David Firestone, "Q. & A. with Anthony P. Carnevale," *New York Times*, December 6, 2013.
15. Caralee Adams, "Latinos, Blacks Strongest Supporters of Increasing College Attainment, Poll Finds," *Education Week Blog*, April 17, 2015. The results, released by Gallup and the Lumina Foundation, were based on 1,533 phone interviews with adults in late 2014.

Chapter 7

The Art of Craft

What is it about working with one's hands that can be so satisfying, even joyous in quiet ways? Here are six satisfying, even joyous thoughts of practitioners followed by an extra point about where the Minnesota Vikings play. As implicit nuggets of career advice, they are intended mainly for young people, but not exclusively, as they perhaps have even greater power for many men and women contemplating midcareer changes.

Ole Thorstensen is a carpenter in Oslo, Norway, and author of *Making Things Right: The Simple Philosophy of a Working Life*.[1]

- "I like my hands; they have been formed by my age and my work. Some scars, none of them large, all the fingers intact, they are my work: carpenter's hands. The skin is hard, yet free of calluses; it's a long time since I have had them. The skin on them is like a thin work glove. My history can be read in them, I think; my hands look like what I have done and do in life. They are a testimonial, my personal CV."[2]
- "One of the nicest things I can say about another person is that we have done some heavy lifting together, and I mean that literally. To hold one end of something heavy and be aware of another's movements, feel them transmitted through the object, is an experience all its own. I can tell if the other person is adept at carrying, if they show me consideration or just think of their own burden, and I can sense when they are getting tired. Fatigue is reflected in their step, in imprecise motions. It is expressed by silence. Anyone who is able ought to lift something together with another person from time to time; it is a good way to get to know one another."[3]

Peter Korn is a furniture maker, an Ivy League graduate whose father wanted him to pursue a *real* profession, and author of *Why We Make Things and Why It Matters: The Education of a Craftsman*.[4]

- "I belong to a generation of furniture makers to whom woodworking initially presented itself as a lost art from a more authentic time. When I turned my first clear pine board into a cradle, and for many years thereafter, I was beguiled by rediscovering the *how* of craft. How do you sharpen a chisel? How do you cut a sliding dovetail? How do you make a chair comfortable? Eventually, though, I also began to wonder about the *why*. What is craft and why does it matter? Why do we make things? Or, more specifically, why do we choose the spiritually, emotionally, and physically demanding work of bringing new objects into the world with creativity and skills?"[5]
- "It was not just making furniture that I loved, but also *being* a furniture maker. I like being self-employed, working hard to meet my personal standards, and trusting in the skill and strength of my hands. Having a storefront location meant having a public presence. Mary the butcher, Mike across the street, the Dominicans who frequented the social club two doors down, and the local artists all knew me first and foremost as a furniture maker."[6]

Matthew B. Crawford runs a high-end motorcycle repair shop in Richmond, Virginia, and is the author of *Shop Class as Soulcraft: An Inquiry into the Value of Work*.[7]

- "Aristotle begins his metaphysics with the observation that 'all human beings by nature desire to know.' [Before going on, have I mentioned that Crawford, in addition to fixing Harleys, holds a doctorate in political philosophy from the University of Chicago?] The special appeal of the trades lies in the fact that they resist this tendency toward more remote control, because they are inherently situated in a particular context. In the best cases, the building and fixing they do are embedded in a community of using. Face-to-face interactions are still the norm, you are responsible for your own work, and clear standards provide the basis for solidarity of the crew, as opposed to manipulative relations of the office 'team.'"[8]
- "There is pride of accomplishment in the performance of whole tasks that can be held in the mind all at once and contemplated as a whole once finished. In most work that transpires in large organizations, one's work is meaningless taken by itself. The individual feels that, alone, he is without any effect."[9]

Less abstractly, you may want to consider football and the temples built in its name. More precisely in this instance, U.S. Bank Stadium in Minneapolis, home of the Minnesota Vikings. While my wife and I now live in a Twin Cities suburb, we lived in Minneapolis when the stadium, which was completed in 2016, was under construction. I'm also good friends with one of its major contractors. At a breakfast meeting with him one morning as the stadium was nearing completion, close to when I finished reading *From Shop Class to Soulcraft*, I began waxing how thousands of men and women had worked on the stadium. And how for the rest of their lives they could tell their children and grandchildren with deep satisfaction, perhaps as they drove by together, "I helped build that."

Whatever one thinks about football, yes, the place is that grand.

As a rule, I stay miles away from proposing that high schools expand their curricula to address assorted lists of societal problems. I've been in meetings, for instance, when participants have said it's essential that students take a required course regarding the personal and societal benefits of marriage. As avid a proponent of marriage as I may be, I've argued against those suggestions on two grounds: Such additions would further clutter what frequently are already overstuffed curricula; and much of what would be taught inevitably would run counter to what people around the table wanted advocated in the first place.

Despite those objections, let me suggest, not a full-fledged course of any kind, but rather modest reading assignments—homework that would barely cover a chapter or two from one or two or possibly three books. For authors, I'm thinking of the just-mentioned triumvirate of Thorstensen, Korn, and Crawford, as some of what they write about routinely isn't taught anymore given the demise of shop classes. The three emphasize the intrinsic worth and beauty of men and women knowing how to use their thumbs expertly, along with their hearts and minds, for endeavors other than texting.

Reading a handful of pages or chapters in their books cannot equate with sculpting real maple or fixing intricate engines hands-on. Yet for large numbers of current students who know very little about molding or restoring, a few brilliant pages about physically demanding and beautiful things could be a revelation.

Back to interviewees. Nate Elifson is the welding student at Minneapolis Community and Technical College we met last chapter. Matthew Nickolay is his friend and an HVAC student at Dunwoody College whom we also met. I had just asked them what they get from working with their hands.

Nate: "I'm just finishing up my first semester of MCTC's welding program, pursuing my A.A.S. degree there. I had never done welding before this year, and I'm enjoying it very much."

I asked why.

Nate: "People had been telling me desk jobs can be replaced by robots, but you'll always need someone to fix your plumbing or electricity as well as weld. That's the 'thinking ahead' reason for choosing welding. But I've always wanted to learn how to work with my hands better. It was never really emphasized in my family when I was a child. But having manual labor skills is a value to me."

Matthew: "I'm in the two-year HVAC program at Dunwoody, which is heating, ventilation, air-conditioning, and refrigeration. I'm currently in my second semester there. I chose it because my friend Richard's dad had been in the field, though he's a pipefitter now. But he always talked to me and Richard about HVAC, and it always sparked an interest in me growing up. My dad was in human resources, and my mom was in the restaurant industry. Doing things with my hands was never something I really learned how to do. This is a brand-new field for me. Kind of echoes what Nate said about his own life."

I prodded the two to go deeper.

Matthew: "It's something you see other people doing, and they can be so talented at it, like welding and knowing how to wire up a house and fix a car. The trades are a different world than the world of restaurants and offices that I'm used to. I like pursuing knowledge and learning about the world around me."

Nate: "I guess I'm studying to become a welder because of the adventurous side of me. My mom was the one who worked with her hands most in my house. She was the one who fixed things when they were broken. My dad was a pastor and didn't really know how to do those things. Out of that, I developed this sense that being a good homeowner and taking care of a house is what men do. A friend, who's also a pastor, said 'The house is a man's fortress, but the woman decorates it.' I think of that as being able to build my own house. But whether I actually build my own house or not, being able to run and maintain it has always been important to me."

At one point, Nate effused about the "black and white beauty of fixing things" as opposed to the grays of various other occupations.

Moving to a new theme, I asked what the two young men thought of what Matthew Crawford, he of heavy-duty biking and heavier-duty philosophizing, says about the comparative intellectual demands of different kinds of work. Or in my paraphrase of his argument, that it regularly takes more intellectual firepower to figure out what ails an engine and then fix it than it takes to perform many white-collar jobs for which four-year degrees are required.

Matthew (Nickolay): "I definitely agree. Next semester at Dunwoody we'll be working more on troubleshooting. You get a call from someone who says their refrigerator is not working, and they need someone to come over. You get there, and it's your job to diagnose the problem, get a new part, and then install it. Figuring out how to get the refrigerator running again is a multistep process. It takes brainpower to piece the puzzle together. Working on situations like that pushes you to think outside boxes."

To the extent both Matthew and Nate too readily downplayed the intellectual requirements of many white-collar jobs in our conversation, it probably was because I located too many of those jobs in "cubicles." It was too much of a leading question. But a better question likely wouldn't have changed much, as they both seem genuinely pleased with the educational and career choices they have made, not that either chap was created for a cubicle, anyway.

We met another student, Lah Htoo, in chapter 2. Born in a refugee camp in Thailand, he was a high school senior in Saint Paul when we spoke, planning for a career in the trades. I asked why he liked working with his hands and when he realized it.

"Since I was little. I like making stuff. I like taking things apart and putting them back together."

I asked what kind of satisfaction he derived from doing things with his hands.

"Seeing the finished product. So if I make something, and it turns out good, I'll be happy about it. If it doesn't turn out good, I'll make it again and make sure it goes well."

Given that the title for this chapter, "The Art of Craft," grew out of a PBS program about cooking with Jacques Pépin, I went looking for something written in which his hands had pride of place even over what he had plated. After a failed but an admittedly cursory search for something apt, I came across the following excerpts in the *Times of India* in a piece titled "Cooking Can Elevate the Soul to Great Heights."[10] It doesn't mention Pépin, but it does convey a complementary, if overheated spirit.

"Food is a universal necessity," author Rudroneel Ghosh wrote, "But it is only human beings who endeavor to transform food into something more."

Cooking is the "most versatile art form and, in a way, a spiritual activity."

A "chef's creative canvas knows no bounds. He has the means to play with the senses, serenade them and often, lead them gently to a higher plane."

And for good measure, "Cooking is perhaps the highest form of meditation, a divine ritual that is key to nourishing the soul and balancing the cosmic forces of yin and yang."

Dessert, anyone?

Which brings us to Darlynn Benjamin and her wonderful cakes, cookies, and chopped vegetables. In my interview with her and her husband Lindsay, she spoke of professionals who tire of their jobs and who've had enough "up to their eyeballs" in the minutiae of their work, and declare, " 'I'm not going to do it anymore. I'm going to . . .'" At which point, I rudely interrupted and asked, "You want to bake pies, right?" Darlynn corrected me by saying it was cookies and cakes topping the list, but her point had been made. I asked why she might make such a big move from social services administration to baking as a new career.

"It's a passion. It's something I like to do. It's something that takes me away from thinking about work. And it's something that's very simple, very easy for me to do. I love to watch the batter come together. And then in the oven, voilà! It's this cake."

"You like working with your hands, I gather?"

"I do, that's why I knit and . . ."

"That's why you chop vegetables," Lindsay jumped in, "when we cook together."

Ivan Charner, an expert when it comes to transitions between school and work, said we've shortchanged people who work with their hands because we inadequately recognize how they "work with their heads and their hands."

Ben Wright, the former president of Dunwoody College who holds a Ph.D. in history, said much the same when I asked how can we do a better job of getting more Americans to have greater respect for people who make their livings working with their hands. "If more people knew the Joel Elftmanns of the world, that would help."

One of the reasons Wright mentioned Elftmann is that we're both friends of his, and we both know something about his remarkable career. "Here's a guy," Wright said, "with a two-year degree from Dunwoody, a tool and die program, I think. He started his shop in his basement or garage, I believe, which is a typical Dunwoody story, and from there developed an incredible international high-tech company, FSI. Not only was Joel good with his hands, not only was he skilled, he obviously became a good businessman. He became a good salesman. He had to, as he had to negotiate with Japanese and other business leaders around the world. He had to learn, but that's a virtue of a lot of Dunwoody people. They're not afraid of learning new things, as that's all part of applied education."

A few moments later, Wright recalled how "Dunwoody used to have a little pin for its graduates that had a triangle on it. We used it to talk about the three points of the triangle: It was the intellect, it was the hands, and it was the heart. It takes all those things to make a great leader, make a great person."

Catrin Thorman is my American Experiment colleague as well as a former teacher with a four-year degree, engaged to a man with a two-year degree plus certificates in information technology. She refers to his "skilled hands, but also his skilled mind" when talking about his love for working on computers, which includes taking them apart. "He has to know how to communicate with his clientele and share with them what could be going on in a way they understand, especially because a lot of times it will be via phone and not in person. So he needs a combination of hard and soft skills."

Dave Svobodny is the hardware entrepreneur we met in chapter 2. I had been relaying a story I had heard a few years prior about a factory that was having a hard time getting something to line up properly with something else, when someone had the good idea of hiring farmers or people who had grown up on farms to fix the problem, which they did. I had recalled the episode because I had been telling Dave how I've long respected, even envied people with farm backgrounds, as they generally learn how to do things with their hands as well as develop strong work habits, a sense of agency and efficacy, and the useful like.

To which Dave said he once told a 22-year-old, "'Take this as a compliment, you're as smart as a 65-year-old farmer.' Farmers have gone through it all, they still have their faculties. They know what's going on. And they know how to fix anything by just looking at it. They carry a vise grip and some baling twine and wire, and they can hear an engine and say, 'Something's wrong there.' And it's fixed."

We'll return to what additional interviewees had to say about the art of craft, but let's digress for a moment to what economist Joseph Schumpeter wrote, as far back as 1942, about the disconnect between people doing "manual work" and the value of the skills and outlooks cultivated in four-year schools.[11] More specifically, Schumpeter had sobering things to say about how the expansion of higher education made life not easier but more difficult for many graduates.

The growth of colleges and universities beyond what the market demanded, he wrote, "creates" for otherwise white-collar workers "employment in substandard work or at wages below those of the better paid manual workers." And that on many occasions, the rise of American institutions of higher learning "may create unemployability of a particularly disconcerting type," as the man "who has gone through college or university easily becomes psychically unemployable in manual occupations without necessarily acquiring employability in, say, professional work." Three-quarters of a century later, it's intriguing to wonder how Schumpeter might update his analysis, if he thought it needing any updating at all.

I note Schumpeter's critique without any digs at American higher education, but on the excerpt's remarkable prescience alone. And because it appears in Matthew Crawford's *From Shop Class to Soulcraft*, a book, more than any other, that led me to write *Education Roads Less Traveled*. I cite Schumpeter also because it's a good spot to celebrate how "manual occupations" means working on *things*, which is no small thing, even if doing so may not have the panache of various other endeavors. "John Dewey's view of the world," for instance, "which is the way you fulfill yourself in the world, especially if you're an American, is by working on things, by doing things."[12] Or, as put more abstractly by a furniture-making philosopher: "We think with materials and objects at least as much as we think with words, perhaps far more. They are conduits through which we construct ourselves and our world."[13]

Back to what interviewees had to say about employing hands, hearts, and minds in the artful and satisfying service of craft—what sociologist Richard Sennett distills as "doing a job well for its own sake."[14]

In talking to Dave Svobodny about the sense of accomplishment in fixing a broken window, I had just noted how Peter Korn, the furniture maker, introspectively reveled in being known as a furniture maker, and I hoped I wasn't sounding patronizing when talking about the "glories of working with one's hands." Evidently, I wasn't, and Dave described how, in the hardware business, "when a broken window comes in, and you fix it in 15 or 20 minutes or in a half-an-hour, it's all good, it's all fixed, you've got that done. You build your confidence with each and everything you fix and build." A few comments later, he spoke of the "biggest thing" that makes him sad in the hardware business.

"A father comes in. He might be 55 or 60 years old. His son, who's in his 30s, also comes in. They're working on a project together. While the son may have a lot of specialized knowledge in his field, he doesn't know anything about how to fix something underneath his sink. So his dad is doing all the talking—not that his son is shy or anything. I know the 'kid,' but I don't know the dad. Then to top it off, the dad pays for whatever they buy. C'mon Dad, you didn't teach him how to use his hands to fix things when he was 10, and you're still not teaching him.'"

From fixing kitchen windows to a story about restoring a state capitol designed by Cass Gilbert, the same architect who designed the U.S. Supreme Court Building: Built between 1896 and 1905, the Minnesota State Capitol in Saint Paul went through a massive restoration and renovation between 2013 and 2017 during which 30,000 pieces of marble were restored or replaced.[15] Who were the masons? As proudly reported by President Rassoul Dastmozd, one of them had graduated from Saint Paul College. I previously had heard there were hardly any masons in the country who did that type of specialized work, a fact which was confirmed by Dastmozd when he said there were only three. Starting off as a "simple mason," the alum "went to Europe, finished his apprenticeship and worked in Italy, France, and Germany before returning home and working on the Capitol."

I know the building well, as I worked there in the early 1980s and visit it regularly to meet with legislators and others. It was a magnificent structure before its renewal and is even more so now. One can only imagine the pride of all the craftsmen who did the hands-on work, especially those who prepared for perhaps the biggest jobs of their lives by studying under Old World masters.

Before closing this chapter on a personal and professional note, what else might we learn from our three, very hands-on craftsmen about the satisfaction and joys of hands-on work? What might young and not-so-young people trying to figure out their future gain by thinking about it with creatively open minds?

Ole Thorstensen, our Norwegian carpenter:

- "Good precision in craftsmanship is not dogma but necessity. I have met a few people in the course of my job who have had a bewildering attitude toward accuracy, almost viewing the need for it as an attack on their personal liberty. They often conceive of themselves as having a particularly well-developed sense of freedom. They 'mix it all into a gravy,' as we say in Norwegian, and think the customs of good craftsmanship is the same as submitting to authority, as kneeling to power. They want to be free to improvise, or as I see it, to do what they want. They will never make good craftsmen."[16]
- "I never feel a greater pride in my profession than when carrying it out alongside [other craftsmen] like these. I know them like I know no one else, in a way I could never adequately explain to anyone other than others like us. They feel the cold, suffer the dust, the same as I, and have a good understanding of what I do. The mutual respect we have would be difficult for outsiders to understand. This cooperation is one of the best things about being a craftsman."[17]

Peter Korn, our University of Pennsylvania furniture maker:

- "As a carpenter, I had worked with my hands. As a furniture maker, I began to work creatively with my hands, which made all the difference. Becoming a carpenter may have been a process of self-definition and self-transformation, but as I gained competence, the daily work of carpentry became a known quantity. Designing and building furniture, on the other hand, has never lost the challenge of exploration and the delight of discovery."[18]
- "Let me be clear: people who are creatively engaged are not necessarily happier, more fully realized human beings than the rest of us. To master a craft is not to achieve a state of enlightenment, despite my youthful expectation to the contrary. Creative practice simply makes our lives richer in meaning and fulfillment than they might be otherwise. For some of us, creative practice may be among the few slender threads that bind our lives together at all."[19]

Matthew Crawford, our University of Chicago biker:

- "Any high school principal who doesn't claim as his goal 'one hundred percent college attendance' is likely to be accused of harboring 'low expectations' and run out of town by indignant parents. This indignation is hard to stand against, since it carries all the moral weight of egalitarianism. Yet it is also snobbish, since it evidently regards the trades as something 'low.' The best sort of democratic education is neither snobbish nor egalitarian. Rather, it accords a place of honor in our common life to whatever is best."[20]
- "My point, finally, isn't to recommend motorcycling in particular, nor to idealize the life of a mechanic. It is rather to suggest that if we follow the traces of our own actions to their source, they intimate some understanding of the good life. This understanding may be hard to articulate; bringing it more fully into view is the task of moral inquiry. Such inquiry may be helped along by practical activities in company with others, a sort of conversation in deed. In this conversation lies the potential of work to bring some measure of coherence to our lives."[21]

As with the half-dozen Thorstensen, Korn, and Crawford excerpts at the start of this chapter, there is no need to romanticize anything about these latter half-dozen, especially since some of the passages do beautiful jobs of that on their own. What the excerpts do suggest, especially for those with inclination and amenable talent, are paths to enriching careers in the crafts. This is the case not just for young people just setting out, but once again, also older women and men possibly thinking about major midcareer (and later) changes for themselves.

A few concluding words, if I may, regarding what my own hands are good for.

I wrote about 500 nearby words on my birthday. Rather than a burdensome way of spending my seventieth, it was a thoroughly satisfying morning and afternoon, as I was approaching the end of the book's penultimate chapter, meaning I was approaching the end of its first draft, which always have been great days in book writing for me.

Some of my most fulfilling moments are steps along the way to a book's publication. Key stages such as refining an idea weighty enough to carry a book. Finding a publisher who agrees. Writing first words. Sending in a first draft. Hearing what editors think. Massaging additional drafts. Reviewing rounds of proofs. Agreeing on cover art. And finally, the day of release. Followed by dinner that evening with my wife at a storied restaurant, in an old part of town, where joyous celebrations are legendary.

As I noted in the book's dedication to the millions of American men and women who create and maintain essential and beautiful things with their hands, the only things I do with mine are eat and type. It's usually a good laugh line, but the longer I write professionally (I started as a reporter in 1971), the more I see writing as my craft and art, and I give thanks for the underlying gift of talent. But frankly, I also give thanks for my discipline and tenacity in developing that gift. So while I'll never have the satisfaction of doing the kinds of brilliant things Thorstensen, Korn, Crawford, and other craftsmen do every day, I have a good sense of what they want the rest of us to know, and why what they do is worthy of respect and celebration.

NOTES

1. Ole Thorstensen, *Making Things Right: The Simple Philosophy of a Working Life* (New York: Penguin, 2017).
2. Ibid., p. 41.
3. Ibid., pp. 99–100.
4. Peter Korn, *Why We Make Things and Why It Matters: The Education of a Craftsman* (Boston: David R. Godine, 2013).
5. Ibid., p. 7.
6. Ibid., p. 45.
7. Matthew B. Crawford, *Shop Class as Soulcraft: An Inquiry into the Value of Work* (New York: Penguin, 2009).
8. Ibid., p. 199.
9. Ibid., p. 156. Personally, suffice it to say I've had a much greater sense of accomplishment working in a small think tank than in a Washington bureaucracy.
10. Rudroneel Ghosh, "Cooking Can Elevate the Soul to Great Heights," *Times of India*, May 22, 2013.
11. Crawford, pp. 129–30.
12. David Firestone, "Q. & A. with Anthony Carnevale," *New York Times*, December 6, 2013.
13. Korn, p. 68.
14. Richard Sennett, *The Craftsman* (London: Penguin, 2008).
15. Todd Nelson, "Restoring Glory: A Balancing Act for Architects on Capitol Restoration," *Finance & Commerce*, August 11, 2017.
16. Thorstensen, p. 171.
17. Ibid., p. 53.
18. Korn, p. 37.
19. Ibid., p. 166.
20. Crawford, p. 32.
21. Ibid., p. 197.

Chapter 8

Conclusion

How much momentum is there, in fact, propelling the education and career options advocated in these pages? Are significant proportions of young people choosing careers for which four-year degrees are unnecessary significantly larger than they were a few years ago? Or hasn't anything changed much? What do actual statistics say? Not what compelling arguments in previous chapters might lead one to believe, but rather, what does hard evidence say?

Here are a few numbers:

- The number of certificates awarded below the level of associate's degrees in the United States grew by almost 500,000 between 2000–2001 and 2010–2011, but they fell by almost 100,000 between 2010–2011 and 2015–2016.
- The number of associate's degrees awarded grew by approximately 365,000 between 2000–2001 and 2010–2011, but they grew by only approximately 65,000 between 2010–2011 and 2015–2016.[1]

For a good spell now, a lot of individuals and groups in the business, education, and nonprofit communities have been busy setting up programs throughout the United States aimed at getting more young people to consider careers in the trades, manufacturing, and other fields in which baccalaureates are not essential. This is what I was referring to when I earlier said there are many impressive education and other activities going on that students and parents don't know enough about, if anything. Yet while such activities are sizable in number, they have not led to commensurate increases in the number of young people choosing to earn certificates and two-year degrees. By extrapolation, these activities have not led to commensurate numbers of students bypassing white-collar jobs to pursue careers working and creating with their hands.

This perhaps is surprising, given what Fred Senn, an advertising veteran who's alert to trends, said in an interview about cultural momentum. Here are several of his comments, interspersed over a boxed-lunch hour.

"Cultural momentum is tremendously important. The last time we had a conversation like this several years ago, it was about family formation and cultural momentum was going the wrong way, making it a desperately difficult problem. But now you come up with this new topic, which, I think, has tremendous cultural momentum. More people are waking up to the notion that we've got to fix our economy." The previous conversation Fred referred to was four years ago when I was writing a book about family fragmentation.

After talking about how a supposed non-four-year momentum resulted from too many young people (and their parents) burdened by too much college debt, Fred continued: "The other source of cultural momentum is the press, the media. They're on to this case. There are more and more articles written about how our colleges are failing us and how we've got to find another solution." Of note, Fred is a trustee of a very good university.

"When somebody throws a fastball at my head, like you do, Mitch, I think about having lunch a decade from now when we're declaring victory on this issue. But what would victory look like? I think the most important thing will be that more people won't feel that their kids must have a four-year degree. And that everybody accepts that."

I said everyone already accepts that, but for *other* people's kids.

To which Fred scaled back his "everybody" and said, perhaps in a bit of fun, "Well, maybe if they have three kids, they'll accept it for one."

All this was early in our conversation. By the time we hit dessert, he allowed: "Boy, I started out by saying you had cultural momentum. I think you do, but . . ." As in conversations I had with a few other interviewees, Fred either let his thought fade away, or I rudely interrupted him. The transcript is not clear on the point. But the implication of his half-sentence was "Who knows?"

My views here about colleges and universities and their possible futures have a fair amount to do with my being more of a gradualist than someone who favors fast, sweeping change. It's also the product of someone whose involvement in higher education, albeit decades ago, was successful and fulfilling, both as a graduate student and as a member of a president's staff. I still find colleges and universities, especially with a few ounces of wine in me, special places. Meaning, I don't agree with people who expect colleges and universities to change dramatically over coming decades. Or just want them to do so because of what they see as the institutions' basic inability and/or determined refusal to adapt to new economic and other environments, with all of it resulting in their diminished ability to serve students and the nation adequately. To be clear, I don't put Fred Senn in that severe camp.

Our nation's colleges and universities, as they currently stand, sometimes totter, and often anger are core American institutions. First established, now rooted, they won't be routed by displeasure and worse over tuition levels, or by frustrated graduates having hard times finding good first jobs, or even by the kinds of ideological assaults on the First Amendment that drive me wild. Masses of students will not choose two-year and certificate programs instead. Enrollments, likewise, will not cave because millions more join the Army or participate in apprenticeships.

Will colleges and universities change, sometimes significantly, because of the crosswinds we've been talking about? Certainly. Will they, for example, decide to coordinate more effectively with community colleges and high schools? Yes, they will. Will enormous numbers of four-year colleges and universities wind up fundamentally reconfigured or defunct? No, they won't, which will be a good thing, as there is no societal profit in taking excessive shots at them.

Do I have proof for all this? Other than an educated faith, no.

Everything argued in *Education Roads Less Traveled* is ultimately in the service of encouraging high school students and others, including parents, at least to consider an education destination other than a four-year college or university and a career for which a four-year degree is not necessary. This would be to the benefit of large numbers of students and of the economy and nation more broadly.

For many young people, considering additional options decreases chances of mistakenly enrolling in a four-year institution that's a poor fit, followed by dropping out, followed by long stretches of unemployment or underemployment, followed by being brought down further by substantial college debt.

Framing matters more positively, giving serious thought to the book's arguments increases the variety of educational institutions and programs a young man or woman might choose from, with many newly discovered paths consuming fewer years of his or her life. Leading, in turn, to smaller opportunity costs and lesser debt and, from there, to well-paying jobs and solid middle-class careers. All this might sound too neat, and given the way the world works, it more than occasionally will be. Yet it's a way of constructing a life that's undersubscribed to the detriment of millions, as well as to the detriment of an economy that crucially needs more people skilled in the trades and many other jobs. Occupations in which heads plus hands are vital.

Is this a route and destination for everyone? The answer to the rhetorical question is, of course not. This is a big country, and many millions of people are built for and prefer different education experiences and then lives afterward. But is it a route and destination for many more people than are now taking advantage of it? The answer to that rhetorical question is, without question.

Yet, different from everything I've read, I've also challenged the attractiveness, especially in the eyes of women, of the kinds of "alternative" education routes and jobs in which men wear uniforms to work and maybe get their hands dirty. There is no groundswell of wondering aloud about how interested women with B.A.s and M.B.A.s might be in becoming romantically involved with men who have A.A.s and certificates. Perhaps one will start here.

There is a similar lack of salience regarding potential racial complexities (make that racial "tensions") involving benign variations on vocationalism on the one hand and, on the other, educators who address five-year-old African American students as "scholars" and explicitly prepare them, from first school bells, for elite colleges and universities, not blue-collar training and jobs.

I raise possible obstacles like these in part because they are inherently interesting, and because they need to be acknowledged and adequately examined if less-traveled education roads really are to be better traveled.

We haven't said much about how issues like these tie into questions of mobility and inequality. I'll leave statistics to others this time around, as the straightforward, and I would like to think reassuring points I want to make don't need any.

Somehow, I've used the term "middle-skill jobs" only twice, but that's how many of the jobs we've been talking about are often categorized—jobs that are much more likely to lead to solid middle-class lives than extravagant ones. This is the case even though substantial proportions of people who choose to make their careers in occupations like these do better financially, often a lot better, than if they had earned a B.A. And given how unimpressively many jobs tucked away in cubicles pay and how well plumbers and electricians routinely get paid, one-year and two-year certificates can be comparatively golden tickets.

But let's also consider men and women for whom the hard decision they must make is not between attending a university or community college but rather between enrolling in a community college and not pursuing any kind of formal education after high school at all. And how, if they pick the latter anti-path, their chances of scrambling and floundering for the rest of their days go up measurably. I've said little about people in situations like these, but when thinking about what certificates, associate's degrees, apprenticeships, and job training in the military might do for them, it's easy to think of such non-four-year routes as pure gold.

Bottom line: There are no guarantees of any kind in these lines of work, as demonstrated in part by how many blue-collar workers have been locked in economic place for a long time. But given a strong national need to replace legions of highly skilled baby boomers, given how mastering a skill is generally more remunerative than not having one, and given that we will continue needing more welders than English majors, I have no hesitation arguing that many Americans will be better served by thinking seriously about, and then pursuing, the kinds of education and kinds of occupations we've been focusing on.

Nevertheless, several interviewees suggested less confidence than the amount I just asserted regarding people being paid enough for a variety of jobs.

In one interview, a man asked: "Are the businesses and industries and captains of industries willing to pay a livable wage?" Which, he said, is not $15 an hour, but "about $20 an hour, with opportunities for lifelong learning." By this, he meant tuition assistance "for a person to go back and get their four-year degree or postgraduate degree."

I asked a woman, "How do we get more young people to pursue these kinds of degrees? To get more of this kind of training?"

"Pay them," she said.

When someone else in the room interjected, "Well, yeah, but it's . . ."

"Pay them," she repeated.

In celebrating people who work in the trades and with hopes of many others becoming proficient in them, I pray it's not terribly sacrilegious to reimagine whose "hands" are referred to in Psalm 138: "Do not abandon the works of your hands." A few ideas about how this might come to be.

A first thing to do is strengthen and expand career and technical education in high schools and in lower grades, too. We've heard several times from Frank Forsberg, a former United Way official with whom I worked when I served as a director of the Greater Twin Cities United Way. In opening our conversation, I asked, "For someone like you who has done so much with workforce issues, what should I know?" And he was off:

> As I think about the topic, it has to do with building much better bridges between high schools—especially public high schools—and the workforce. It has to do with much more smartly utilizing high school time to build skills and credentials for real jobs that young people can see and touch and feel. In really great situations, high schools would be partnered with local businesses and local technical and community colleges so that pathways for students were seamless and easy.

At which point, I asked about the kinds of courses students would take.

> Students are still going to need great math skills, which they're failing to learn right now. They also need to be competent in other traditional subjects and skills. When I think about this topic, I start by thinking about "middle" kids—kids

> who may not be on a college track, or at least not obviously on a college track, but who are open to having a meaningful high school experience. Starting in ninth grade, they would take a mix of classes with more hands-on courses than usual. I envision opportunities within businesses such as internships and apprenticeships. Ideally, their parents would be engaged in this endeavor.

Frank then said what I hope will be the case:

> I'm assuming your book and other conversations like this will trigger a rebalancing of what's available in high schools, with the kinds of shop classes I remember as a high school kid adjusted to be more relevant to the technical skills required in today's job market.

How best to push needles for this and similar purposes, starting with getting young people to more frequently consider education routes other than those on four-year autopilot, as well as careers other than what they and their parents had instinctively assumed would be sought?

- Interviewees talked about taking much larger advantage of ever-increasing social media platforms. Rarely, though, will anyone older than 25 or 30 (I'm being glib but not by much) have an adequate clue about how to do this, as chances are they won't know what electronic means of communication and persuasion are in or out for what age-group or another. Then there is the need to reach parents, which can require significantly different approaches and vehicles, electronic and otherwise. In each instance, hire and contract smartly.
- Interviewees also talked about celebrating the accomplishments of kids whose focus is on CTE and doing so as vigorously as we celebrate kids whose eyes are set on the Ivies. This is a lovely and worthy goal that I endorse, not that I see it happening in my lifetime. But we can make progress. Similarly, we need to better celebrate the accomplishments of men and women who later earn A.A. degrees and certificates.
- Matthew Crawford, the philosopher biker, urges college students to use summers to learn a trade and earn a certificate. It's a great idea. As is learning a trade by earning a certificate after earning a B.A. or B.S.; a decision that may well prove to be a lifesaver at various points in a person's life, financially and in other ways.
- Especially in chapter 3, there are descriptions of programs across the country seeking, one way or another, to train young and older men and women for jobs in manufacturing and the trades, thereby increasing the number of highly skilled employees required by businesses and industry. This is especially important given the rapid retirements of baby

boomers—programs such as Tennessee Promise, Kentucky Fame, and the Central Minnesota Manufacturing Association. One of the things I've learned over the last two years is there are many more such programs and efforts under way around the country than I had imagined. This is not to say we don't need additional strong ones, because we do.

- Programs like these also can play a bigger role in trying to train, not only eager and willing workers, but also people, disproportionately men, who have dropped out of the workforce entirely. Demographer (among other things) Nicholas Eberstadt wrote in 2016, "In the half-century between 1965 and 2015, work rates for the American male spiraled relentlessly downward, and an ominous migration commenced—a 'flight from work,' in which ever-growing numbers of working-age men exited the labor force altogether." Adding up numbers like these, Eberstadt concluded, "America is now home to an immense army of jobless men no longer even looking for work—more than seven million alone between the ages of 25 and 55, the traditional prime of working life."[2]

  The economic as well as social and cultural crisis Eberstadt describes—all exacerbated by opioid and other addictions—is megatonnage more difficult than everyday mismatches between job requirements and job skills. But again, that's not to say the kinds of programs cited a moment ago couldn't help, because they could.

- An even more complex problem distorting the American economy is massive family fragmentation and the enormous degree to which it leads to educational deficits, increased mental illnesses, higher incarceration rates, and other shortcomings and losses. It's easy to say community colleges, apprenticeships, and military training programs can do many things, but significantly reducing unmarried birth rates and divorce rates is not one of them. But to the extent they can help make more men (and women) successfully employed and, therefore, marriageable, they definitely can.
- A consistent lament in the book is the incapacity of high school counselors to provide students with sound advice and encouragement about careers in technical areas such as manufacturing and the trades (as well as agriculture, broadly construed, not that I've said anything about it). This certainly is worrisome, perhaps even angering, but not surprising, given how school counselors routinely have very large caseloads composed of significant numbers of teenagers with significant family, mental health, and other adolescent problems. In addition, relatively few school counselors know very much about technical fields and issues, as they overwhelmingly were education and liberal arts majors themselves. This is a big problem.

  My argument is less with school counselors and more with the failure of other players in education, business, and industry to step in. I suggested in chapter 3 that business officials—and not only in human resources—could offer advice to high school students, not on campus but in nearby community centers or, perhaps even better, in logo-emblazoned trailers parked across the street or around a corner from school. I met with an official of the National Association of Manufacturers who proposes the same thing.

- Also regarding improved counseling is the need for many students, starting in high school, to have a better grasp of just how much it will cost, month after month, to pay back $10,000 or $25,000 or $50,000 or more in college loans (plus interest) and to start doing so sooner than they might imagine. How to better illustrate the kinds of big financial, family, and other problems that can be caused by big money bites? Many school counselors and others are already describing postcollege economic facts of life conscientiously, even energetically. But how to drive them home even more vividly?
- Most comprehensively, how best to change the very culture? By objective analysis, passionate advocacy, and perpetual communication. Or in more direct language, leaders in education, business, government, and other fields who believe more students should consider non-four-year routes to good jobs and good careers need to speak up more and write more, and then repeat, repeat, and repeat.

Are these ideas as weighty and compelling as the problems they are meant to address? Probably not. But recommendations at the end of books about tough issues usually sound weak in comparison. Or if not weak, then over the top romantically.

Permit me to bring the chapter and book to a close, first with the help of my late brother-in-law, David Holder, then with the help of my main mentor, C. Peter Magrath. And then with the help of a woman I have not met but who captures what work means, especially if our aim is trying to help young people: Nancy Hoffman.

I interviewed David in November 2017 in Garland, Texas, a day after the wedding of one of his four children, a daughter. His health clearly was not good at the time, and he was to die two months later, at 66. A good man he was. He was a successful and exceptionally well-respected insurance adjuster, and our conversation was the kind that doesn't seem to be on-target at the time, but after rereading the transcript several times, it becomes clear that it frequently was perfectly on point. Which is to say he describes how dramatically things had changed when it comes to the kinds of education and credentials—or lack thereof—a person must have to enter and flourish in a profession that, in this instance, was his for almost four decades. I opened by asking what he did for a living:

> I am an independent insurance adjuster specialized in heavy equipment, tractors, and trailers. "Independent" meaning that I work for a number of insurance companies, and my job is to go out in the field and examine the tractor or trailer or piece of equipment after an insurance claim has been made on it. Fire, theft, spoilage of food, or whatever the insurance covered.
>
> Many people with whom I work are qualified more because of their experience than because of their education. They understand the equipment. They understand the people who are repairing it. They understand the market. The majority of these adjusters don't have a college education.

David then moved on to the "people who actually make the repairs":

> I've been doing this for the last 38 or 39 years. Times have changed. The people in the repair shops, the older guys generally, they're not college educated. They have learned what they do through experience. I liken their craft to art, in what they're able to repair, re-create, imagine, and bring back to life. The guys who worked for the insurance companies may have had a little more education because they were required to write reports and so forth. But they had to be able to understand and communicate with the fellas who actually were doing the work and there had to be a rapport between them.
>
> The adjusters in the field, such as myself, we would talk on the same level as the repair people, and there were great and fluid relationships between us. Adjusters also talked to truck drivers, owner-operators, people who operated machinery, and a majority of these people also were not college educated. If you came off as something better because you had an education, you were frowned upon, and they weren't going to open up to you and divulge the secrets of the trade.
>
> The best guys in my field were the guys who came from the repair shops and learned what insurance was all about. They could build relationships with the repairers, vendors, and everyone else. Those guys could communicate. They knew what was happening on shop floors. And they knew how to talk to the managers, who also generally had come from the floor.

Let the record show that my brother-in-law was one of those "English majors" that Senator Rubio evoked, with a B.A. from Trinity University in San Antonio.

"There was a great deal of resistance by the old-timers when I first started doing this. They were my mentors. They were my teachers. But I had to prove I was willing to listen, understand, and appreciate them."

David proceeded to talk about what it means that both adjusters and repair shop managers are now expected to have four-year degrees and how important dynamics have changed because of it. Here's one passage:

> I'm talking to young, college-educated men and women at insurance companies, and I'm trying to explain why it's going to cost their firms hundreds of thousands of dollars to do something, and I relate it to a specific type of equipment. They haven't a clue what I'm talking about. They have a preconceived idea of what their job is, intellectually, but they're not communicating with real people out there—with truck drivers, machine operators, repairers. As for college-educated managers of repair shops, they often don't have experience on the floor and don't understand how things actually work, either.

Beyond its personal meaning, how does this replay of my conversation with my late brother-in-law mesh with the book? It's not that neither David nor the book views four-year degrees as the one, true educational credential. Rather, it's how the economy and businesses of all kinds have changed significantly and how it's increasingly hard to think of any field in which formal educational credentials of some sort—some might say for good or ill—aren't essential. And while young people hoping to land good jobs and then build good careers might not need a B.A. or B.S., it's close to imperative they earn *something* solid. Which is where the educational routes we've been talking about lead to.

I've mentioned that I worked for Peter Magrath in the 1970s when he was president of both Binghamton University and the University of Minnesota. He later went on to become the president of the University of Missouri system and the (then-named) National Association of State Universities and Land-Grant Colleges. From there, he served as interim president at West Virginia University, and then had another stint as president of Binghamton University. And he's currently writing a book of his own, far from his first.

We talked about my book at an Irish bar in Glen Echo, Maryland, not far from where he lives with his Episcopal priest wife, Susan. (I've mentioned, haven't I, that my wife Diane is Episcopal clergy, too?) It was in this spirit that Peter said, "Well, maybe it's a question you've discussed, but I don't think we have, and it's implicit in what you're working on: What about things that make people happy inside their soul? I think I could give an answer to that."

"Let's do," I said.

"What is it that makes human beings have a sense of self-worth, happiness, and exhilaration? It's when we do work that is fulfilling and we're working with people. When we're working with others whose company and companionship we enjoy." He strongly implied that academic degrees are of lesser import.

I told him I tease matters like that early in the book when I write that most people, I assume, would be happier if they had a job that really enthused them but that paid a little less money, rather than have a job where enthusiasm and money were the other way around.

"That's right," he said, adding, "I think my answer is, you know inside your heart, your soul, your innards, what it is that makes you happy."

The trip from there is short to what Nancy Hoffman, a vice president of Jobs for the Future in Boston, writes about working for a living[3]:

> To do productive work is a fundamental human need. Work supports families, promotes the well-being of communities, and ensures the health of the economy. Work attaches citizens to the public sphere. Work also helps individuals form strong identities and enables people to act in the world. Why would a society not want to support young people directly finding good work and learning to do it well as insurance for their future prosperity and stability?

I certainly don't have any arguments with that. Or with what David and Peter said. Or with what the great majority of the more than 80 generous people who sat for interviews generally had to say either.

America's fixation on four-year-college degrees speaks to an egalitarian impulse, which in real ways, is impressive and good. But it also makes it unduly difficult, sometimes impossible for many young people to pursue their strongest interests. It also makes it hard to take advantage of their innate gifts, the fruits of which are crucially needed by our nation. For all concerned, it would be big step forward if education roads currently less traveled were better traversed.

NOTES

1. U.S. Department of Education, National Center for Education Statistics, Higher Education General Information Surveys (HEGIS), "Degrees and Other Formal Awards Conferred" surveys; and IPEDS Fall 2000 through 2016, completions component. My thanks to Nicole Smith of the Georgetown University Center on Education and Workplace for help in tracking down pertinent data.
2. Nicholas Eberstadt, *Men Without Work: America's Invisible Crisis* (West Conshohocken, PA: Templeton, 2016).
3. Nancy Hoffman, *Schooling in the Workplace: How Six of the World's Best Vocational Education Systems Prepare Young People for Jobs and Life* (Cambridge, MA: Harvard, 2011), p. 23.

Index

A.A. degree. *See* associate's degree
A.A.S. degree. *See* associate's degree
American Technical Education Association, 22, 68–69, 87–88
apprenticeships, x, 4, 5, 11, 15, 23, 35–36, 46–50, 53, 55, 57, 66, 77, 80, 82–83, 87, 93, 106, 113, 114, 116, 117
associate's degree (A.A. degree or A.A.S. degree), x, 6, 7, 9, 15, 25, 47, 48, 57, 60, 68, 77, 81, 83, 87, 93, 101, 111, 114, 116. *See also* two-year degree

B.A. degree. *See* bachelor's degree
bachelor's degree (B.A. degree or B.S. degree), x, 1, 3, 7, 8, 9, 11, 12, 15, 16, 23, 24–26, 28, 30, 32, 47, 48, 52, 62, 65, 67–68, 69, 80, 81, 85, 87, 88, 90, 94, 114, 116, 119, 120
Banaian, King, 26–27, 50, 78, 89
Banks, Ralph Richard, 92–93
Benjamin, Darlynn, 88–89, 94, 103–104
Benjamin, Lindsay, 38, 50
Binghamton University, 3, 10, 21, 62, 120
Bird, Caroline, 21
Brookings Institution, 8, 25
B.S. degree. *See* bachelor's degree

career and technical education (CTE). *See* technical education
Carlita, 59–60, 91
Center of the American Experiment, 8, 13, 43
certificate, 1, 2, 4, 5, 6, 7, 9, 15, 23, 27, 31–32, 36, 46–47, 48, 49, 51, 56, 57, 60, 63, 66, 68–69, 77, 79, 83, 87–88, 91, 93, 94, 97, 98, 104, 111, 113, 114, 116; distinction from certifications, licenses, 46–47
certificate program. *See* certificate
certification. *See* certificate
Charner, Ivan, 10, 49, 104
City University College Center at New York City Community College (CUCC@NYCCC), 3
class and race, 12, 13, 16, 32, 83, 85, 92–93
college debt. *See* debt
college enrollments, 9
community colleges, 9, 10, 11, 12, 15, 16, 23, 24, 29–30, 39, 47, 52, 73, 83, 87, 90, 91, 113, 114, 115, 117; and avoiding debt, 59, 63, 69

craft, 1, 35, 48, 49, 50–51, 53, 99–109, 119, 123
Crawford, Matthew, 5, 48, 100–102, 105, 108, 109, 116
CTE. *See* technical education

Dastmozd, Rassoul, 29–30, 41–42, 88, 96, 106
Davis, Mitch, 41, 60–61
debt, ix, 8, 15–16, 26, 30, 31, 50, 52, 56, 57, 59–73, 83, 88, 91–92, 112, 113
Department of Education, 10, 11, 86
Department of Labor, 5, 36
Dunwoody College, 45–46, 65–66, 92, 101–102, 104
Dynarski, Susan, 63–64

Eberstadt, Nicholas, 54, 117
economic growth, 16, 73, 79
educationally mixed marriage, 2, 3, 13, 16, 30, 83, 85–98
Elifson, Nathaniel, 92, 101–102

Finn, Jr., Chester E. (Checker), 10, 26, 68, 96
Fleming, Kevin, 5
for-profit educational institution, 6, 59–60, 63
Forsberg, Frank, 6, 53, 97, 115
four-year college bias, 21–33
Freed, Gwendolyn H., 23

Georgetown University Center on Education and the Workforce, 2, 5, 96
G.I. Bill, 9–10, 15, 23
Gray, Kenneth, 11
Griffith, Amanda, 66–67
guidance counselors. *See* school counselors

Hanushek, Eric A., 79
Harvard: Business School, 80; Graduate School of Education, 24, 80; report, 7, 96
Higgins, Marilyn, 54
high school (guidance) counselors. *See* school counselors
Hoffman, Nancy, 46, 118, 121
Htoo, Lah, 31–32, 103

Jerrim, John, 11, 23
Josh, 59–60, 91

Kaiser, Kent, 52, 71n7
Kaylee, 59–60, 91
Kerry, 60, 91
Kersten, Katherine, 43–44, 53–54, 57, 82
Korn, Peter, 17, 100, 101, 106, 107, 108, 109
Kornecki, Dave, 96
Kresbach, Sandra, 22, 48, 68–69, 87–88

Lerman, Robert, 4–6, 35–36, 47–48
license, 6, 46–47
licensing. *See* license
loans, 14, 15, 16, 26, 48, 59, 61–62, 64, 67, 78, 118; defaults, 63; federal Perkins, 62; federal PLUS, 62; federal Stafford, 62
Lumina Foundation, 7

Magnuson, Roy, 32, 41–42
Magrath, C. Peter, 21, 118, 120
marriage, 2, 3, 13, 16, 30, 60, 83, 85–98, 101, 117; associative, 86, 91; and class, 16, 85, 93; and debt, 59–60, 91; educationally mixed, 2, 3, 13, 16, 30, 83, 85–98; of equals, 86, 91
McGee, Mike, 38, 49–50

McGowan, Rev. Diane Darby, 37, 86–87
Michels, Bob, 55
military training, x, 11, 15, 23, 29, 48–49, 64, 77, 80, 87, 93, 98, 114, 117
Miller, Darlene, 42, 45, 73–75, 77–78, 87
Minnesota Chamber of Commerce, 79, 82
Minnesota State University system, 26, 38, 49, 51
Morphew, Christopher C., 23
Moser, Myron, 42, 56–57, 75, 77–78

National Association of Manufacturers, 74, 117–18
National Center for Education Statistics, 6, 67
Nation at Risk report, 7, 15, 39
Nickolay, Matthew, 92, 101–102
Norman, Amanda, 30–31

Obama, Barack, 45, 73
occupational certificate. *See* certificate
Olson, Gen, 40
one-year certificate. *See* certificate
Owen, Stephanie, 25–26

PBS, 1, 103
Pell Grants, 56–57
Pépin, Jacques, 1, 15, 103
Peterson, Scott, 51–53
Pogemiller, Larry, 29, 69–71
President's Council for Jobs and Competitiveness, 45, 73
professional certificate. *See* certificate
Project Build Minnesota, 50
Putnam, Robert D., 86

race and class, 12, 13, 16, 32, 83, 85, 92–93
Renn, Aaron M., 2
Risdall, Ted, 55
Roloff, Tori, 62–63
Rosenbaum, James E., 11, 23–24
Rubio, Marco, 5, 35, 119
Ryan, 60, 91

Saint Paul College, 29–30, 41–42, 45–46, 88, 96, 106
Samuels, Don, 94–96
Samuels, Sondra, 94–96
Sawhill, Isabel, 25–26
school counselors, ix, 15, 17, 22, 23, 24, 42–43, 82, 117–18
school debt. *See* debt
Senn, Fred, 48–49, 69–70, 112–113
Shop Class as Soulcraft: An Inquiry into the Value of Work (Crawford), 5, 100–101
shortages of skilled workers, 6, 11, 50, 73–76, 78–79. *See also* skills gap
Siegel, David, 78, 88
skills gap, 75–76, 82. *See also* shortages of skilled workers
Slama, John, 69–70
St. Cloud State University, 26–27, 50, 89
Star Tribune, 2, 4
STEM (science, technology, engineering, and math), 2, 68, 76
Stout, Stacey, 79, 82
student loans. *See* loans
Svobodny, Dave, 27, 46, 105, 106

technical college. *See* technical education
technical education, x, 1, 4, 6, 7, 11, 12, 16, 17, 22, 24, 27, 28, 29, 30, 36, 38, 39, 40–44, 49, 54, 56, 74, 76, 77, 83, 93, 96, 115, 116; and avoiding debt, 63, 65, 66, 67
technical school. *See* technical education
Thorman, Catrin, 43, 60, 104–105

Thorstensen, Ole, 17, 99, 101, 107, 108–109
trades, x, 16, 17, 23, 24, 31, 32, 35, 37, 38, 41, 42, 47, 48, 50, 51, 54, 73, 74–75, 83, 85, 87, 88, 94, 95, 100, 102, 103, 108, 111, 113, 115, 116, 117; unions. *See* unions
Trostel, Philip, 2–3
two-plus-two programs, 47
two-year certificate. *See* certificate
two-year degree, 1, 4, 5, 24, 25, 30, 51–52, 59, 60, 63, 66, 70, 87, 88, 89, 104, 111; and income, 25, 66, 70, 87. *See also* associate's degree

unions, 15, 17, 32, 43, 47–48, 53, 83, 86, 93
United Way, 6, 53, 96–97, 115
University of Chicago, 5, 100, 108
University of Michigan, 63
University of Minnesota, 3, 21, 26, 40–41, 120
University of Virginia, 62
U.S. Department of Education. *See* Department of Education
U.S. Department of Labor. *See* Department of Labor

VET. *See* vocational education
vocational education (and training), ix, x, 2, 7, 12, 13, 15, 17, 24, 39–41, 46, 57, 65, 93–94, 96

Wake Forest University, 66
Webber, Douglas A., 66–67
Weerts, David J., 23, 26
Wright, Ben, 65–66, 67, 104
Wright Technical Center, 44
Wyman, Nicholas, 5, 35

Yellen, Janet L., 93–94

Zill, Nicholas, 86, 91, 98n4

About the Author

Mitch Pearlstein is founder and former president of the Center of the American Experiment, a think tank he and a small team of colleagues started in Minnesota in 1990. Now senior fellow with the Center, his other books include *Riding into the Sunrise: Al Quie and a Life of Faith, Service, and Civility* (2008); *From Family Collapse to America's Decline: The Educational, Economic, and Social Costs of Family Fragmentation* (2011); and *Broken Bonds: What Family Fragmentation Means for America's Future* (2014). He holds a doctorate in educational administration from the University of Minnesota and is married to the Rev. Diane Darby McGowan, deacon at St. George's Episcopal Church in St. Louis Park, Minnesota. They have four adult children, seven grandchildren, and two aging rescue dogs, Trevor and Bailey, who still derive as much joy digging with their paws as the craftsmen in these pages derive from working with their hands. Home is Eden Prairie, Minnesota.